CHANGING CONTEXTS OF OUR FAITH

LETTY M. RUSSELL, *editor*

FORTRESS PRESS   **PHILADELPHIA**

COPYRIGHT © 1985 BY FORTRESS PRESS

Library of Congress Cataloging in Publication Data

Main entry under title:

Changing contexts of our faith.

Bibliography: p.
1. Theology—Addresses, essays, lectures.
2. Ethnicity—Religious aspects—Christianity—Addresses, essays, lectures. 3. United States—Church history—
20th century. I. Russell, Letty M.
BR50.C43 1985   277.3'0828   85–4418
ISBN 0–8006–1862–9

1712A85   Printed in the United States of America   1–1862

CONTENTS

Contributors   5

Foreword   9
    Jeffrey Gros

Introduction   13
    Letty M. Russell

1. Exploring the Context of Our Faith   21
    Letty M. Russell

2. Expanding Horizons: Coming to New Consciousness
   as a North American   36
    Barbara Brown Zikmund

3. Retelling the Story: Reinterpreting Biblical Tradition
   as a Woman   49
    Kathleen Farmer

4. Transforming Suffering: Struggling with Life as an
   Asian American   63
    Roy I. Sano

5. What is Contextual Theology?   80
    Robert McAfee Brown

Suggestions for Study and Action   95

Additional Resources   109

CONTRIBUTORS

JEFFREY GROS, F.S.C., is Director of the Commission on Faith and Order of the National Council of Churches of Christ in the U.S.A. He has a B.A. and an M.Ed. in biology education from St. Mary's College, Winona, Minnesota; an M.A. in theology from Marquette University, Milwaukee, Wisconsin; and a Ph.D. in theology from Fordham University, New York, New York. Brother Jeffrey taught for several years at high school, adult ministry training, college, and seminary levels. He also served on diocesan ecumenical commissions and on the board of the National Association of Diocesan Ecumenical Officers.

LETTY M. RUSSELL is Professor of the Practice of Theology at the Yale University Divinity School, New Haven, Connecticut. She was ordained to the ministry in 1958 by the United Presbyterian Church, U.S.A., and served as a pastor and educator in the East Harlem Protestant Parish for seventeen years. Her books include *The Future of Partnership, Growth in Partnership*, and *Becoming Human* (Westminster Press). She is active in the Faith and Order Commission of the National Council of Churches and of the World Council of Churches.

BARBARA BROWN ZIKMUND is Academic Dean and Associate Professor of Church History at Pacific School of Religion, Berkeley, California. She is ordained in the United Church of Christ and represents that denomination on the Commission on Faith and Order of the National Council of Churches of Christ. In 1983 she attended the Sixth Assembly of the World Council of Churches as an accredited visitor. Before coming to PSR in 1981 she taught at the Chicago Theological Seminary. Her most recent books are: *Discovering the Church* (Westminster Press, 1983) and *Hidden Histories in the United Church of Christ* (Pilgrim Press, 1984). Dr. Zikmund holds degrees from Beloit College, Beloit, Wisconsin, Duke Divinity School, and Duke University, Durham, North Carolina.

KATHLEEN FARMER is Associate Professor of Old Testament at United Theological Seminary in Dayton, Ohio. She is of native American heritage and grew up in western Nebraska. She holds degrees from the University of Nebraska and Southern Methodist University (Perkins School of Theology). She has written curriculum resources for Graded Press (the United Methodist publishing house) and has conducted a number of seminars and workshops for both clergy and lay education. She is presently preparing a volume on *Proverbs and Ecclesiastes* for the Wm. B. Eerdmans Publishing Company's new International Theological Commentary series.

ROY I. SANO is an Asian American. His parents come from Japan and he was born in Brawley, California. He has pastored in rural and urban churches, and has served as a chaplain and teacher at Mills College, Oakland, California, and the Director of PACTS (Pacific and Asian Center for Theology and Strategies). He has also taught theology and Pacific and Asian American ministries at Pacific School of Religion, Berkeley, California. He authored *From Every Nation Without Number*, an exploration of ways to promote racial inclusiveness in the church, and *Outside the Gate*, a study of the Epistle to the Hebrews for United Methodist Women. He is a bishop in the United Methodist Church assigned to the Denver area.

ROBERT MCAFEE BROWN is Professor of Religion at Pacific School of Religion, Berkeley, California. He has been a member of the Faith and Order Commission of the World Council of Churches since 1975. Among his many writings, those dealing in more detail with the implications of contextual theology, are: *Theology in a New Key: Responding to Liberation Themes* (Westminster Press, 1978); *Gustavo Gutierrez* (John Knox Press, 1980); *Creative Dislocation: The Movement of Grace* (Abingdon Press, 1980); and *Unexpected News: Reading the Bible with Third World Eyes* (Westminster Press, 1984).

FOREWORD

As Christians seek a deeper unity around the world and between Protestant, Catholic, and Orthodox, they plumb their own experiences more profoundly as well as those of their fellow believers in other traditions. The richest ecumenical experience for those in local church communities is often that of sharing the context of their own personal faith with those of churches, cultures, races, and experiences different from their own, resulting in a broadened horizon. In facing the commonalities and differences of the Christian faith, the Faith and Order movement attempts to provide resources for this kind of sharing.

It is hoped that this book will be useful for study groups of local congregations, paired and clustered communities of Christians, covenanted churches, and communities where ongoing dialogues between churches have been studied. It offers an instrument for examining the effect our world environment has upon us and our faith. The experience of Christians participating in ecumenical dialogue has more to do with the bringing together of persons from different cultural contexts than with the abstract exchange of universally understood theological options. Thus, this exercise of examining our context prepares us for actual ecumenical encounter by helping us come to understand how our faith is shaped by our own particular world and how the limitations of our particular context make it difficult for us to understand persons shaped in other world contexts.

The book provides opportunities for Christians to deepen their bonds of unity with one another and to expand the vision and method by which they see the gospel relating to their own lives, the lives of persons in other faith or societal communities, and to the issues of the modern world. For this reason, the Commission on Faith and Order is most happy to provide this short introduction to a method of relating our faith to our context.

In the past, the Faith and Order movement has helped parishes involve themselves in *Living Room Dialogues* (New York: Friendship Press and Paulist Press, 1970) and *The Community of Women and Men in the Church* (Philadelphia: Fortress Press, 1982). Likewise, current discussions around the world and in the United States on the issues of "Baptism, Eucharist, and Ministry" and dialogues between pairs of churches are enhancing the efforts toward better understanding of our faith as it is practiced by Christians of varying traditions. Over the years, as a movement, Faith and Order has raised up issues of differences between us in questions of morality, sacrament, Scripture and tradition, and church practice. The development of a better understanding of our own and one another's context will hopefully deepen our desires to make the experiences of others a part of our own spiritual lives.

At present, there are small groups of Christians around the world gathering together to look at their own experience and to look at the wider context in which they live in order to become active agents for the unity of the church and the renewal of human community. To further the goal of this ecumenical ideal, groups who study this volume might consider reaching out to find those in their community with whom they would be least likely to be in dialogue.

Finally, the Faith and Order movement is grateful to Christians in the United States for their enthusiasm in ecumenical collaboration, prayer and spiritual life, and active ministry. We hope that this volume provides a reflective moment in that zeal for Christian mission, for which the church exists, and which the ecumenical movement has been called to serve. The unity of the church is the gift of God for the sake of the world. If this study assists us in our local context, making the world we live in a larger place, and helps make our faith better understood by one another, then we will be gratified.

BROTHER JEFFREY GROS, F.S.C., *Director*
Commission on Faith and Order
National Council of Churches of Christ
in the U.S.A.

INTRODUCTION

LETTY M. RUSSELL

At one time or another in our lives most of us have been afraid that our faith will be swept away by the floods of change. A crisis or sickness or death; the loss of someone we love; a change of job, finances, or living situation may cause us to question God and the meaning of life. Usually we do not find any easy answers to our questions, but sometimes as we begin to heal and adjust to new circumstances we recognize that our faith has grown and deepened, rather than been swept away by change.

One reason this happens is because faith is not some superficial form of right knowledge or action, for faith, like love and hope, is a relationship of trust in God that is not reducible to any one form of knowledge or action. This relationship of trust in God springs from the very core of our being and is capable of growing and changing as we grow and change.

The greatest risk to our faith from changing contexts and circumstances is not that it will be swept away, but that our relationship with God will not be allowed to grow and change as we are faced with new situations. Like all relationships, our relationship with God needs to be nurtured and cultivated. When it is ignored, what happens is not that we lose faith but that it gradually ceases to shape our life, actions, and knowledge. Faith is a gift of God that needs to be used, a talent that must be invested. In this book on *Changing Contexts of Our Faith* the writers want to help us understand how changing contexts can become occasions for new knowledge and faithful action.

GOD'S GIFT OF FAITH

The most basic reason that faith is not swept away by the floods of change is because it is a gift of a God whose promises are faithful. Through the community of the church, we hear the story of God's love and we experience God's self-revelation as one who cares for us and for all humanity in Jesus Christ. In response to God's self-revelation we "fall in faith." Whether sudden or gradual, this conversion experience turns our life around so that we see ourselves, our neighbors, and the world through the perspective of God's concern for the mending of creation. And we spend the rest of our lives trying to find out how we can become what God intends us to become, full human beings in partnership with God in the care of one another and of the creation.

Another reason that the relationship of faith seems to endure many crises is that those who practice the presence of God are continually nurturing different aspects of that relationship. For instance, the Bible does not give just one description of faith. The different descriptions seem to include at least three elements: knowledge, action, and trust. Sometimes in our lives one or another of these is very important in our relationship of love with God, and they are never all present in the same way. We may be at a loss in one aspect while full of faith in another way. For instance, faith as knowledge of the story of God's love in Jesus Christ is important because it helps to know and understand the one we love and try to obey. But that knowledge, like all our knowledge, grows and changes with our age and ability and with the church and social context in which we find ourselves.

In the same way, we know that our actions of faithful response to Christ's call to follow him always fall short of our own intentions and God's hopes. Yet we often act in response to our neighbor's need in a way that surprises us and opens us to new knowledge. Our actions on behalf of personal and social needs are very much part of our faith, but they do not make or break our relationship to God. That relationship is a free gift from a God who is trying to love us into becoming fully ourselves, by giving us a chance for imaginative and constructive repentance when our actions fall short of God's expectations.

INTRODUCTION

There are times in our lives that all we can hang on to is the trust that God loves us in Jesus Christ, no matter what. There are other times that we cannot "find God" and our experience of trust is more of a memory than a reality. When this happens we are often living out our faith through our actions, or joining others in studying the Bible and thus living our faith through our doubts. God does not give up on us, even when we seem to have lost God, and for this reason faith is a powerful reality in our lives, which like the love of God is a rock amidst the floods of change.

FAITH IN CHANGING CONTEXTS

Although our faith is more likely to become rusty from lack of use than to be swept away by crises and change, it does change as contemporary contexts change. That is, our understanding of God's love in our life changes as we are changed by our life experiences. The gift of faith does not change, but the way we live out our new relationship with God in Jesus Christ is a continued story. This book is an invitation to Christian readers from many different traditions and church backgrounds to share in an exploration of the ways faith can be nurtured in the midst of change. Changing contexts are opportunities for new knowledge and faithful action when we risk opening ourselves to the questions and perspectives they bring.

All of the chapters in this book include conversion stories of the way minds and actions were changed because of exposure to new situations and opportunities for dialogue with new partners. The opening chapter by Letty M. Russell on "Exploring the Contexts of Our Faith" uses personal stories and biblical materials to explain the way our perspective on reality influences what we see, hear, understand, and believe. The interaction between faith and context is described in regard to the influences of social, church, and theological contexts on the way we understand and live out our faith relationship of trust with God.

Barbara Brown Zikmund's chapter on "Expanding Horizons" describes her own shift in perspective which came about through participation in the Sixth Assembly of the World Council of Churches at Vancouver, Canada, in the summer of 1983. In her description of coming to consciousness as a North American, she tells about the difference it has made to her to see things from the perspective of Christians living and witnessing to their faith in other parts of the world.

Kathleen Farmer's chapter on "Retelling the Story" helps us see how biblical tradition needs reinterpretation in the light of new perceptions of the roles of women and men in church and society. The rising consciousness of women and the feminist interpretation of the Bible has led her to respond to her daughter's questions about the call of God with answers that are different from those her mother would have given her.

Roy Sano shares a story of his own "conversion" through working with Christians struggling for human rights and democracy in South Korea. Through the witness of their faith in "Transforming Suffering" he came to a new vision of the world in which he lived and in turn was led to studies of social, biblical, and theological materials that could provide a new basis for faith in action as an Asian American.

Last of all, Robert McAfee Brown describes what it is like to change your mind about the way you go about the theological task of thinking about God. In a chapter based on his speech to the Commission on Faith and Order in San Francisco in the spring of 1982, Brown helps us understand how faith is incarnated in our own context and life experience. He makes a special plea for the legitimacy of theological reflection that begins with experience rather than abstract categories. Brown's chapter on "What is Contextual Theology?" helps us to look back at the sharing in the first four chapters, and to realize that all the authors not only wrote about how new contexts changed their understanding of faith, but also wrote about what Brown describes as contextual theology.

The "Suggestions for Study and Action" provide a variety of ways to use this book for study in congregations, in ecumenical groups, and in social action task forces. Along with suggestions and questions, this section contains a model for Bible study in context. In many ways this is a do-it-yourself book that illustrates how the authors have grown in faith through exposure to changing contexts, and invites the readers to discuss their own examples of faith in changing contexts.

The book itself is a product of such a do-it-yourself study on "Contextualization" by a working group in the Commission on Faith and Order of the National Council of Churches of Christ. This group met as part of the ongoing work of the Commission from 1982–84. In studying the impact of contextualization on the understanding and interpretation of the Christian faith, they decided to look at three case studies. The three stories presented by Zikmund, Farmer, and Sano represent final versions of our case studies. This book itself is not a report of what we learned. Instead it is a workbook for those who would like to share with us in the continuing task of relating faith and action.

WAYS PEOPLE CHANGE

We know that people change very slowly. Even a sudden change or conversion experience is usually a dramatic recognition of what has been happening inside of us for some time. Our fear of change comes from the recognition that the changes in our world happen much faster than our own faith and understanding. Often we cannot cope with change and go into what is called *culture shock*. At this point we cannot function in our situation very well and don't understand what is going on, just as if we were suddenly in a new culture and language in another part of the world. In moments of culture shock we are not able to change at all because our way of understanding ourselves and the world no longer makes sense and we don't know what to do. Certainly we experience such moments as unpleasant, risky, and threatening. Yet we ourselves can grow and develop in our faith and understanding of the world if we are patient and try to live through the moment of crisis and learn from it. Such crises can become for us what James Loder has called "transforming moments."

Change can be risky, not only because we may find that we "cannot cope," but also because a great deal of change is for the worse. As we face accidents, ill health, old age, domestic and public violence, injustice, technology with potential for destruction of the earth, and an unending list of change for the worse, we are certainly glad that nothing can separate us from the love of God (Rom. 8:38). But when we seek to grow in faithfulness in every circumstance, changes in our world and in our experiences challenge us to live out our faith relationship with God and our neighbor in new ways.

There are two particularly important ways we mature as persons through changing circumstances. The first is through what is called *cognitive dissonance.* When the way we think about things and understand them no longer makes sense of what we are experiencing, there is discord or dissonance between the way we think and our actual experience. When the situation makes no sense, we may go into culture shock. When it makes some sense because it is still connected with our past ways of knowing and we are challenged to new ways of thinking, then we will grow in faith.

The second way we are helped to change for the better, and to grow in faithfulness, is by other *persons who are peers* who may have a more accurate description of our reality and ways of coping with it. Peers are persons like ourselves. The ones most helpful to us in nurturing our faith are those who have additional insight and knowledge to share with us but are not so different from us that we cannot understand their perspective. We like to emulate the superstars in our lives, but we are most helped in our faith journeys by those with whom we have shared similar circumstances at home, work, or church, in study or action groups—day by day.

As we read this material on the changing contexts of our faith we will be reading the stories of persons we do not know, yet the very combination of similarities and differences in their experiences may provoke us to discuss and consider the way our faith is shaped by particular situations. There is no one way of cultivating faithfulness in changing contexts, but I will suggest three ways that might be helpful as we all join in this do-it-yourself process of faith development.

One clue is that we will be open to the way God's Spirit might be guiding us through unexpected circumstances if we cultivate *advent shock.* Advent shock is maladjustment with the present because of the hoped-for future. Alvin Toffler has told us that change produces a form of culture shock called "future shock" in which persons are maladjusted with the present because of the longed-for past. But Christians should always be dissatisfied with the present because of their longing for God's promised kingdom of justice, peace, and wholeness in the world. This most certainly would be a good description of what was happening to Roy Sano as he tried to make sense of the gospel in the face of the suffering that is taking place in many Third World nations and communities. If we look at new contexts so as to seek out signs of the coming kingdom of God and to respond in ways that God would intend, then we will discover new things about what our relationship of trust with God is all about.

Another clue to faith development in changing contexts is that we are more likely to *act our way into thinking*. That is, new occasions *do* teach new duties. They teach us to act differently and to question our old opinions, prejudices, and ways of doing things when we experience cognitive dissonance. An important way to keep growing is to do new things and go to strange places. Exposure to different church traditions, different cultures, and different political and social perspectives is usually more effective through personal contact than through reading or television. Sometimes it is the other way around and thinking leads to action, but often new knowledge is not easily transferred into action and our commitment to act in faithful ways does not keep up with our rhetoric. For instance, it was not just reading feminist interpretations of the Bible that changed Kathy Farmer's response to her daughter. It was her life experiences and actions that led her to reinterpret the tradition for a new situation.

Finally, our faith relationship may be deepened by *listening to the losers of society*. What they have discovered is that the gospel really is good news for the poor, for the downtrodden, for those in despair. They are helping us to read the gospel story with new eyes and to hear interpretations of the Christian faith from a new set of peers. Both Barbara Zikmund and Bob Brown encourage us to listen to the voices of those who have been on the underside of society because these voices from women, from the poor, from people of color, from the voiceless in every place will enrich our knowledge of the meaning of the gospel. Listening to those who are not taken seriously in our own churches and groups and in other parts of the world may help us to discover God's wisdom out of the mouths of those of "no repute" (1 Cor. 1:26–31).

Changing contexts in our lives continually challenge us to grow in faithfulness to the gospel of Jesus Christ. These changes cannot detract from our relationship with God which is built on trust in God's love as well as knowledge and action on behalf of God's concerns for mending creation. What they can do is help us to celebrate the ways we have "fallen in faith" with God, and to join with others in seeking out what that faith might mean for living in these days.

1
EXPLORING THE CONTEXT
OF OUR FAITH

LETTY M. RUSSELL

At the beginning of 1984 the First Congregational Church of West Haven, Connecticut got its first glimpse at the new Peters map of the world. This map shows the oceans and continents in a different perspective because it has been drawn to show all areas according to their actual size.[1] The church was having a family night potluck supper and the speaker was Thomas Paton, a missionary on furlough from Japan. He pointed to the Peters map and asked, "What is different about this map?" A little kindergarten boy spoke up, "Russia isn't cut in half!" At age five he was already used to seeing maps with the United States in the middle and Russia divided on either side. All of us are accustomed to maps that focus on our own particular self-interest. For instance, the popular Mercator projection, drawn in Germany in 1569, shows Europe larger than South America although it is actually only one-half as large. It places Germany in the middle of the map, and countries of North America and Europe appear much larger than they really are.

Maps are not the only things that show us reality from the perspective of our own self-interest. Almost everything that we see on television, read about, or hear about is slanted according to the view of the speakers or writers, and is received according to our own view of things. This leads us to be suspicious of the news we read or hear. Yet we seldom notice that we are also biased in the way we interpret events. In fact, we are all biased. We all see things as large or small, good or bad, important or insignificant from the perspective of our own context or situation. This is why we need to keep checking with a variety of maps and sources of information in order to be aware of the larger picture.

Some of us do this by reading the Bible along with the newspaper; by listening to visitors from overseas as well as our neighbors; by studying or consulting the "experts"; or by traveling to different areas of our own country or of the world. We are aware that it is important to know what is happening around us so that we can make decisions about our lives. When these decisions are matters of faith we turn to the church to help us understand the meaning of the gospel for our daily actions. But, even here, the meaning and interpretation of the Christian faith is affected by the particular theology, tradition, and social situation of the interpreters. This is one of the reasons that people attend so many different kinds of churches. Each tradition brings a different interpretation of the one gospel message.

How do we find out the real truth about our faith in God in today's world? There is no one way because the truth we seek is not an abstract principle, but a person who is "the way, and the truth, and the life" (John 14:6).[2] And the truth we live is not a fixed rule, but a life of faithful response in God in ever-changing circumstances. Yet we can discover more clearly how Christ is present in our pilgrimage of faith if we learn to look at our faith in context. Exploring the context of our faith helps us to sort out the various perspectives that inform the way we see Jesus, both the perspectives of the original stories and their interpretations, and our own perspectives drawn from our present stories and interpretations. Just as Jesus was born a Jewish male, living in a particular time and place, the good news of God's love that his story conveys comes to us in very particular circumstances. Exploring the context of our faith helps us hear that good news more clearly by noticing the way it speaks a word of truth in ever-changing contexts.

There are many ways of explaining what we mean by context. Robert McAfee Brown has suggested at least three meanings that are important for interpreting our faith.[3] First, context is the *surrounding textual material* that helps us understand the full meaning of a particular message. We know that a message gets distorted when it is taken out of context. Second, context is the *surrounding circumstances* or events that led to the formation of a particular message in the Bible, a church creed, or some other document or speech. Knowledge of circumstances helps us understand why a particular message was formulated and what it intended to say. Third, context includes our *contemporary circumstances* as readers, listeners, and interpreters of a particular message. Our own setting affects the way we receive or do not receive a message.

Our reading of the message of faith received from the Bible or church tradition is coded by our social context as women and men, rich or poor, urban or rural, old or young, and so on. It is also coded by our church context as persons of faith in a particular tradition, and by our future context or hopes for the future of ourselves, our family, and the world. Attention to these social, church, and theological contexts of our faith can help us understand the variety of interpretations of faith as different persons explain what Jesus Christ's love means in their situation. Just as the Mercator map of the globe distorts the world to suit the perspective of those living in Europe in the sixteenth century, our "faith maps" often distort the meaning of the biblical message as we suit it to our own social, political, cultural, and church contexts. But like the Peters map, our "faith maps" can become more accurate as we seek to hear the word of God's love in a wider variety of contexts.

OUR SOCIAL CONTEXT

Recently I had the opportunity of expanding my world horizon by traveling to Japan and Korea under the sponsorship of the National Council of Churches of Christ, U.S.A., the National Christian Council in Japan, and the Korean Association of Women Theologians. My trip took me through Hawaii where I visited the War Memorial at Pearl Harbor, viewing the pictures of those who had died and visiting the sunken remains of the USS Arizona in the harbor. I thought of my own childhood experiences of World War II, and of our national outrage at Japan's attack and anguish at the loss of so many lives.

While in Japan I went with Aiko Carter, Secretary of the Women's Committee, National Christian Council of Japan, to the Peace Park in Hiroshima. Here I saw the pictures of the atomic bomb destruction, looked at the few charred remains gathered in the memorial museum, and talked with Aiko about her childhood anguish at being bombed out of her home in Tokyo. I also talked with A-bomb survivors who continue to live in anguish and terrible suffering from the radiation. Whichever way we look at it war is hell! Peace can be the only solution to such devastation. Aiko and I visited the peace statue dedicated to the children who lost their lives from the atomic blast. We wanted to join countless others in hanging little cranes on the statue as a prayer for life and peace. We had no paper with us to make the cranes, but I suddenly realized that I had a world map taken out of the airline's magazine on my flight to Japan. Quickly we picked out our own parts of the world and fashioned our small offering for peace. So far apart in context, we were together in our understanding of God's will for peace with justice in this planet earth.

The social context that separated me from Aiko included differences of culture, race, nationality, language, and political history. We could communicate with each other as long as we remained aware of the way our social context shaped our lives. Out of this awareness came an ability to translate the meaning of our Christian faith so that it could be shared together. This translation required not just Aiko's amazing fluency in English but also attention to the stories of our lives and how these stories colored our perceptions. The same sentences, phrases, or events in our lives looked quite different to those who have seen them from the other side. Yet attention to our own social, political, and cultural backgrounds helped us find unity and mutual understanding, and provided an opening up of our own worlds so that we could see things from different sides.

When we study the Bible we often read about the surrounding circumstances of a particular teaching or story, and our Bible study guides regularly acquaint us with the wider context of a particular passage. But, sometimes, we fail to realize how our contemporary circumstances color the way we read the text. For example, Justo and Catherine Gonzalez have pointed out in *Liberation Preaching* that we often need to "reassign the cast of characters" in a story in order to understand it more clearly.[4] In the familiar story of Jesus'

call to ministry in Luke 4:16–30 we see him standing in the syna-
gogue at Nazareth reading from Isa. 61:1–2 and declaring, "The
Spirit of the Lord is upon me" (4:18–19). Reading this from a white,
middle-class context we usually think about people being called to
ministry. Thus this passage is a popular text for ordination services.
Yet those who read it out of a context of poverty or oppression think
about the words that follow, about preaching good news to the
poor. We cannot get the full impact of the story without asking
what the poor fisherfolk of Solentiname, Nicaragua, hear in this
message, as well as what middle-class preachers, and many other
groups, might hear.[5]

The same is true for the other part of the story. The townspeople
in Nazareth are horrified at the blasphemous claim of this home-
town boy, and they seek to throw him over a hill at the edge of town
(Luke 4:28–30). The cast of characters usually includes us with Jesus
and those rejected for their prophetic ministry. We seldom stop to
consider whether in our own context of comfort and affluence we
may be those who are rejecting Jesus and his message of liberty for
the oppressed. Changing the cast of characters and looking at how
the story changes its meaning according to social context expands
the horizons of our faith and opens up new insights into paths of
faithfulness.

Attention to our social context may feel risky because it
challenges our world view and causes our faith maps to take on new
dimensions. But, just because such risk and struggle help us to
grow in our understanding of God and the world, this is *a good way
to do our own theological reflection*. Our thinking about God is
always contextual because it never happens in a vacuum. Our Christian faith is incarnational. God has chosen to be Emmanuel ("God
with us"), and we can only find God by sharing life with God.
When we honestly let God into our life, we do not find someone
else's answer to faith. We find our own growing faith. We find our
response of trust in the One who loves us enough to share life in
all its weakness, struggle, and death, and at the point of our struggle we find the meaning of hope and life.

A critical examination of our own context is not only the beginning of confession and commitment. It is also the beginning of

unity. As we grow in a critical understanding of how our context shapes our faith, we begin to understand the perspectives of those in different circumstances, and begin to share a common account of our God's love affair with the world.

OUR CHURCH CONTEXT

In the 1960s I shared in a group ministry in the East Harlem Protestant Parish in New York City. Those were difficult but exciting days as we struggled together to live out the meaning of liberty for the oppressed in solidarity with the Civil Rights Movement. Unlike many pastors, I did not have to worry about preaching on social involvement of the church because the interracial congregation had long since made a commitment to service of its community in the struggle against poverty, racism, government corruption, and crime. We were engaged in a campaign for the right of East Harlem citizens to participate in redesigning the map of their community through urban redevelopment, as well as in campaigns for school integration and quality education. But such tasks flowed from the worship and the Bible study groups of the churches. Often the texts would come alive in a new way as a particular crisis helped us see anew the way God was with us so that nothing could separate us from God's love. The Bible study, worship, and action were all an expression of our faith pilgrimage together as a church.

In such a context it was clear that the Bible did not have all the answers. In fact, much of what it said seemed inadequate for the problems we faced; for instance, sayings about slavery (1 Cor. 7:21), or relations of church and government (Mark 12:4), or on divorce (Matt. 19:3). Yet the Bible continued to speak to us in ministries of worship, education, and action. The stories of the Bible were told, compiled, and preserved in the first place because they spoke to the real needs of the communities out of which they grew. Their ability to speak to basic questions of life gave them authority as an authentic word from God and about God that could help shape lives.[6] They continued to speak to our small community in East Harlem, not with answers, but with a promise of God's presence in the midst of oppression. The Bible often records the way God speaks to people in the midst of suffering, despair, exile, and poverty. Here it came alive among a people who continued to "walk through the valley of the shadow of death" (Ps. 23:4).

In this situation the biblical promise of liberation for the oppressed was a lively word. But gradually at the beginning of the 1970s I became more and more aware of the way the Bible and the Christian tradition were not a lively word for many women. As I became involved in the women's movement I began to make connections between the blights of racism and sexism in our society, and I began to look at the Scriptures and traditions of the church in a new way. I saw that these traditions had been, and still were, used to keep women in their place, and I began the process of reinterpretation in the light of contemporary circumstances. This in turn raised the question of how the Bible and the teachings of the church continue to be authoritative when our understanding of the biblical world and of our own world is radically altered by new experiences.

I noticed that such reinterpretation in the light of new situations is not unheard of in the Bible. For instance, the book of Deuteronomy is a revision of the Mosaic law to make it relevant for urban life in the time of King Josiah around 621 B.C. The need for consolidation of sanctuaries, revision of laws, renewal of religious life in the light of the teachings of the prophets and of the new political situation of Israel called forth a reinterpretation of the tradition out of which the people of Israel found life (2 Kings 22—23).

In the same way Jesus reinterprets the Scriptures in the story of his resurrection appearance to two disciples going to Emmaus (Luke 24:13–35). Luke tells us a story of what happened along the road as a very sad couple are returning home, perhaps after following Jesus to Jerusalem to celebrate the Passover. It appears that they are so preoccupied with their own grief that they do not have the faith to discover their missing Lord as he makes himself known in interpreting the Scriptures. By having Jesus interpret his own suffering, death, and glory in the light of the Old Testament, Luke sets a precedent for biblical interpretation and preaching by his followers in every age as they go on reinterpreting the story. The early church was concerned to show all those who are "slow of heart to believe" that Jesus was truly the Messiah, the anointed Savior of God's people (24:25). For this reason their preaching and teaching, like that of the Lord on the road, usually included references to the fulfillment of the promises of God.

The church continues to tell and retell this story, not only because it helps provide a guideline for reinterpreting Scriptures in the light of the resurrection, but also because it proclaims the promise of Christ's presence among us as we break bread in his name (24:28–35). This is a presence that points us to God's promise of love which transcends even the power of death. The presence is of One whose story is known to us in the life, death, and resurrection of Jesus of Nazareth, yet that presence continues to be experienced differently in new encounters along the road of life.

But new experiences are not nearly as radical as that of the disciples who discovered that their Lord was risen indeed! The story of the church is a witness to this new experience of the power of Christ's presence in the lives of Christians in every generation and nation. The biblical witness to the power of God's love and the continuing witness of the Christian community are authoritative, not because they are unchanging, but because they continue to speak in ever new ways. "Jesus Christ [is] the same, yesterday, today, and forever," but what is the same is not the words of his story but the reality of his presence in the life of the faithful through the power of the Spirit (Heb. 11:8b).[7] Christ is the same, but the church and the community of faith are not the same. They keep changing in every time and place and we must reinterpret the meaning of Christ's presence anew in each setting.

Attention to church context, along with other contexts, may provide *a new way of doing our own biblical interpretation.*[8] In the church context we are used to continual reinterpretation of the gospel message through study, preaching, worship, and action. God's traditioning action in handing over Jesus Christ into the hands of coming generations and nations continues through our life, and we are called to participate in this action by witnessing to God's love in Jesus Christ.[9] Sometimes our church traditions help to make this witness by giving us a common heritage and strong identity as a particular community of faith, but at other times these traditions may block our sensitivity to other Christian communities or to the challenges of our social context. Yet they can provide guidelines for us as our own stories of faith continue to change and evolve. Studying the Bible in the light of the church context raises questions about the relation of God's traditioning action in Jesus Christ to our church traditions and customs and helps to open our eyes along the road of life to the challenge of his presence.

When Christian feminists seek to reinterpret the Scriptures and church traditions so that the new situation of the community of women and men in the church is made clear, they are not denying the authority of the message of the Bible or the traditions. Rather they are keeping the message alive so that it can continue to witness to God's love for all humanity in new contexts. They are providing a new opportunity for understanding the meaning of the gospel so that the word can get out and be heard. In short, they offer a new chance for change in the church.[10] The authority of the Bible flows from its authoritative witness to God's saving and liberating presence in history. It evokes our consent to struggle with its story because of that witness. And it invites our continuing pilgrimage to find out what that story means. As Phyllis Bird has put it, the Bible is the church's book because the Scriptures

> are the place where the church hears God speaking and discerns God's presence when their words are studied and pondered and questioned—and opened for us by the Stranger who accompanies us on our journey and breaks bread with us.[11]

OUR THEOLOGICAL CONTEXT

When we take our social and church contexts seriously as a beginning point for exploring our faith, we are confronted by a great deal of diversity. In fact, it seems as if "anything," or, at least, "any context" goes! Yet the diversity of experience is not a denial of our common unity of Jesus Christ. Such diversity is an authentic basis for unity, for it allows us to discover the many ways our Lord can be known to those who attend to the Scriptures and break bread together. The variety of our faith maps affords us with a much richer expression of our one faith in Christ, and leads us to expect Christ's presence in many unexpected contexts. This expectation of Christ's coming into our lives is what provides a third context for exploring our faith and for the expression of our unity in diversity.

It is the theological context of God's promise of New Creation that provides the meaning and hope through which we interpret the events of our life and world now.

In our world, moving so fast toward possible destruction, the theological context in which we find ourselves is not one of hope, but rather one of apocalyptic doom over nuclear destruction, over the collapse of our food chain and life support systems, or over some other technological wonder turned into an instrument of destruction. The old American frontier optimism about infinitely expanding resources and opportunities has begun to fade as we reach the limits of our ecological and political resources. In this context children and adults alike are more likely to consider suicide. Our concern becomes not how to understand the world but how to find hope in a world that is closing in on us. The world maps, and even those of space, no longer tell us where to go to escape this circle of fate.

When human beings find themselves unable to cope with their world and to have some control over their own future, they often find that their whole view of reality changes for the worse. In a sense their world closes in and there is no opening to future and possibility. This can be seen in extreme situations of imprisonment when people give up and become living dead persons who simply go through the actions of life. Or it can be seen in hospitals where people give up the will to live, or hope for recovery. Even when persons are not in any danger, sickness, pain, and disability will still constrict their world and limit their horizon.

This was my experience a few years ago when I lost the sight in one eye in a freak accident. Even as I lay in the hospital thinking about home, I could not imagine how I would function there. Everything seemed to be too much effort. I could barely cope with speaking to those who came to visit. Getting through each minute and hour and day was a total occupation. There *was* no future context to speak of, even though I talked of recovery. Like other seriously ill or injured persons I was living in a survival context and all my other worlds had contracted into that.

The symbol of this was my great fear that I could never again cross the street in front of my house. Without being able to see well, how was I going to keep from being run down by a car if I ventured forth? This fear stayed with me even on my return home and I would play its scenario over and over in my mind. The dangerous street symbolized the physical and psychological constriction of my world view. When I finally was able to cross the street it was no "big thing." I just did it because I was on the road to health.

Each of us has had these experiences of our world view shrinking in the face of physical, social, or psychological pain, for our perception of the world and our situation is directly related to our ability to interact with that world in a purposeful manner. In the light of this we can see why it is important to find a theological context that does not act as a self-fulfilling prophecy of doom. No matter how bad the future may appear, it is God's promise of hope that can allow us to function with courage and compassion. Without this context of God's promise, our personal worlds tend to contract so that we can no longer see the wider picture of our neighbor (and of creation itself) in need.

The importance of hope in God's promise as a source of meaning and insight in our lives has been recognized for centuries. Long ago, for instance, Abraham is said to have "believed against hope, that he should become the father of many nations; as he had been told" (Rom. 4:18). In the same way Jeremiah hoped against hope as he spoke to the discouraged exiles in Babylon and urged them to hope in a God who had plans for them, "plans for [*shalom*] and not for evil, to give you a future and a hope" (Jer. 29:11). This way of looking at the world in the perspective of God has sustained many generations of people who held fast to the promises of God and stubbornly worked toward the fulfillment of those promises.

The words of Jer. 29:10–14 remind us that we are not alone but share this hope with those who have lived through the crises of past history. Much of the prophecy of Jeremiah during the sixth century B.C.E. is one of doom for Judah at the moment when Jerusalem is about to fall. Yet this message to the Jews of Northern Israel, already captives in Babylon, is one of hope in the midst of despair. It is a strange message because he tells the Jews to settle down in their country of exile and build homes, work, worship, for God intends for them to be there a long time. "Don't go around crying and feeling sorry for yourselves. Get on with the business of life," says Jeremiah. He tells them that God has not forgotten the promise and that, in the future, God will return them from exile. They are on God's calendar. There is a plan for them and they have a future and hope.

The basis of Jeremiah's promises to the exiles of long ago was the convenant between God and Israel that God would be faithful to the people and show steadfast love toward them, and that the people were to be faithful and steadfast in their love of God. Jeremiah saw God's punishment of Israel and the fall of Judah as part of that covenant faithfulness in which God spoke out against injustice, strife, and unfaithfulness among the people. The prophet reminds the exiles that they have *a memory of the future* based on their experience of the past. God had been faithful to the covenant, delivering them from slavery, bringing them to a new land, and teaching them how to be faithful. On the basis of this memory Jeremiah can point to the future promise of God that is consistent with the past.

Jeremiah also saw that people could continue to worship and serve even in a strange land without the temple and the familiar landmarks. As he puts it: "You will seek me and find me; when you seek me with your whole heart" (29:13). The old organizations and structures were not necessary for faith because, even in situations of great suffering, God's relationship of love was still there so that people could live in the present out of their future context and find new ways to love and serve.

Today we also live out of the memory of God's future that informs the present. Our hope for solving problems in our personal lives and in the world is not based on confidence in our own ability, nor on a dangerous mixture of technological knowledge and political domination. Our hope is in God's concern for the mending of society and all creation. We remember that in God's plan the lame walk, the blind see, and the outcasts and oppressed of society are included so that they can have hope in shaping their own future (Matt. 11:2–6). As we think about what God's concern for mending creation means in our lives we are doing our own theology. Our future already begins as we make God's order of new and mended creation part of our daily struggle for peace, justice, and human fulfillment. Wherever we are, no matter what our circumstance, we can "build our own houses" and "seek the good of the city"; for in Christ we already belong to God's new order, God's future context. As Paul puts it,

> If anyone is in Christ, there is a new act of creation; the old has passed away, behold the new has come (2 Cor. 5:17).[12]

Our theological context is not just concerned with salvation as what happens when we die or when the new creation of God is fulfilled. It has to do with what Dorothee Soelle calls "life *before* death."[13] For our expectation of the future breaking into our lives now as the presence of Christ both disturbs and comforts us, transforms our present existence, giving it meaning and purpose. Opening ourselves to Jesus Christ means sharing together with others in his life style, not just waiting for the end. This is a life style of service in solidarity with the poor and the outcasts of society. It is choosing to be with those who are sick, persecuted, and oppressed in order to discover how Christ is present there protesting the denial of life. Our theological context becomes the impulse for life before death in the present, in the assurance that nothing, not even death itself, can separate us from God's love (Rom. 8:39).

God's promised future is also a fundamental basis for Christian unity. Whatever may be our differences of tradition and culture, we share in a common memory of the future. We can give a common account of the hope that is in us because we know that one day we will be made one in Jesus Christ (2 Pet. 3:15). In its search for unity in matters of life and faith, the Faith and Order Commission of the World Council of Churches found that this future context was the only one that could include all the voices of crying for hope in a world of despair. In "A Common Account of Hope" written in Bangalore, India, in 1978 the Commission sought to encourage members of Christ's body "in every place" to share in one hope.[14] In attending that meeting I remember just how conscious I was of the narrowness of my own world view as a white North American Christian in an Indian context.

Unity could not come from any sort of homogeneity, but it could come as a result of meeting, living, worshiping, and working together as we struggled to become a community that could share in one common account of hope in Christ. The Commission had been working since 1971 to determine the meaning of Christian hope in a wide diversity of situations around the world in order to give contemporary expression of the meaning of Faith. The final account is not just a verbal affirmation. It reflects the life stories of countless Christians. As we gathered in small groups and began to listen deeply to the many different accounts, and shared them together in critical reflection, we began to hear a common theme. We heard not only "a symphony of groaning humanity" but also "a symphony of hope against hope" in a God who does not forget (Rom. 4:18).

The study of hope was not lightly undertaken. It represented a way that opened up the search for unity in the face of confessional diversity. Even if the churches were not yet ready to make a common creedal confession of faith, they might together find a way to a common account of hope on the long road of realizing our unity in diversity. At the same time, it represented a way opened up in the face of cultural diversity in many political, economic, social, and religious situations. As those who had been marginal to the discussion of theology began to be heard, new forms of shared theological dialogue began to develop, so that new voices of women and men from local and regional settings could be included in the ongoing discussions.

The cultural and confessional diversity out of which an account of hope was shaped in Bangalore represents the diversity of context out of which we all can seek to explore our faith. Beginning with our own contexts and including the context of others in designing our faith maps is not an easy task, but it provides a rich opportunity for new insight and growth as Christians. It also takes our own particular circumstances and differences seriously so that we can understand the way our faith is incarnated on our own setting.

Our contemporary circumstances affect the way we discern God's presence in our lives. By giving critical and careful attention to our social context we can understand our own world view and that of others more clearly. By struggling to understand our church context we will be able to see points where that context is most in need of reinterpretation in the light of new experiences that lead to new understanding of the gospel. Our theological context opens up *a new way of exploring our faith* based on the hope that we have in

God's promised future of new creation. Such hope can transform our actions in the present as we seek to anticipate God's intention for the mending of creation, beginning with us!

NOTES

1. Arno Peters, *The Europe-Centered Character of Our Geographical View of the World and Its Correction* (Münich-Solin: Universum Verlag, 1979; Cincinnati: Friendship Press, 1984).

2. Unless otherwise noted, Scripture quotations in this volume are from the Revised Standard Version. Brackets indicate a word change.

3. See chap. 5 below, Robert McAfee Brown, "What is Contextual Theology?"

4. Justo Gonzalez and Catherine Gonzalez, *Liberation Preaching* (Nashville: Abingdon Press, 1980), 74–78.

5. Ernesto Cardenal, *The Gospel in Solentiname*, 4 vols. (Maryknoll, N.Y.: Orbis Books, 1982).

6. Sharon H. Ringe, "Biblical Authority and Interpretation," in *The Liberating Word*, ed. Letty M. Russell (Philadelphia: Westminster Press, 1976), 27.

7. Brown, "What is Contextual Theology?"

8. Letty M. Russell, *Human Liberation in a Feminist Perspective — A Theology* (Philadelphia: Westminster Press, 1974), 72–80.

9. See "A Model for Bible Study in Context," p. 102 below.

10. Betty Thompson, *A Chance to Change: Women and Men in the Church* (Philadelphia: Fortress Press, 1982).

11. Phyllis Bird, *The Bible as the Church's Book* (Philadelphia: Westminster Press, 1982), 107–8.

12. My own translation.

13. Dorothee Soelle, *Choosing Life* (Philadelphia: Fortress Press, 1981), 47–60.

14. "A Common Account of Hope: Bangalore 1978," *Sharing in One Hope* (Geneva: World Council of Churches, 1978).

2
EXPANDING HORIZONS

Coming to New
Consciousness as
a North American

BARBARA BROWN ZIKMUND

In Greek the word *horos* means boundary or limit. From this root comes the word "horizon," a word we use to describe the edges of our living space. A horizon is that point where the earth and the sky meet. Horizons are the places of sunrise and sunset. The same root is part of the word "horizontal," referring to that which is parallel to the horizon.

Horizons are very personal. Every person, every nation, every event has its horizon. And these horizons are always dependent upon the position of the observer. My horizon in California is different from the horizon of someone in New York or in Germany. Our horizons are different, not because the sky or the earth change, but because each of us lives and views the world from a different place. Every perspective has its unique horizons.

Several years ago when I made the decision to relocate in California I told people that I was moving to the "west coast." Now that I am here, I find that I did not move to the west coast, but that my home is on the eastern rim of the Pacific Ocean. It is the same place, but I understand it differently. I am defining this place in a new way because my perspective has changed. I am seeing horizons I had never noticed. In a real sense we are able to name where we are only because of what we see on the horizons. It is important, therefore, to notice horizons.

A horizon can be precisely defined from any particular place and time, but it cannot be known precisely. I can be part of my neighbor's horizon, but I can never capture the essence of my own horizon. This is why horizons are frustrating, because when we try to capture them, they keep moving further and further away. Horizons also depend upon our capacity to see. Sometimes even when we stand in the same place we discover new horizons that we had never noticed.

Horizons may hem us in or beckon us onward. They remind us of our limitations and invite us to stretch and grow. We dare not ignore our horizons. Horizons can often show us new ways to escape from our earthbound parochialism.

VANCOUVER: WHERE MY
HORIZONS EXPANDED

I am a white Anglo-Saxon Protestant American woman. I grew up in a middle-class urban family in Detroit. As far back as I can remember we always were active in church. Consequently, I came to believe that voluntary church work was important. I learned to give my time and money to support the church. As a historian I also know that my church is part of the long and impressive history of Christendom, stretching back to the ancient world. I am proud of the impact that Christianity has made upon the world: inspiring reform, uplifting primitive peoples, and sharing the good news of Jesus Christ.

In 1983 I was asked by my denomination to be an accredited visitor to the Sixth Assembly of the World Council of Churches in Vancouver, Canada. It was an honor. When the WCC had met in Evanston, Illinois in the early 1950s I had been totally unaware of that Assembly, even though I lived only three hundred miles away. Now I rejoiced that many leaders of churches would be coming to my part of the world.[1]

Upon arrival in Vancouver, however, I was confronted with the reality that Canada, not the United States, was hosting the Assembly. I was a foreigner in a foreign land. I had to use strange money, I had to wait my turn, I could not take any credit for the efficient and warm hospitality offered by Canadian churches. From the very beginning the Assembly forced me to confront the limitations of being an American. I was also pushed to understand my faith in a new context.

At Vancouver I met many Christians who did not speak my language, look like me, or even have some of what I had previously assumed were Christian values. In this multiracial and multicultural setting I was called to sort out what was essential to Christianity and what was dependent upon local language, culture, and habit. It was a life-changing experience because it challenged many of my previously unexamined preconceptions and habits.

I learned to be patient and to let the life of the meeting find its own rhythm. It was a big group and it took time for all of us to be "present." The opening sessions were filled with pageantry and speeches. As the initial enthusiasm waned everyone settled down for the coming eighteen days. Soon thereafter, however, the Americans began to get impatient. "All we do is sit and listen to speeches." "When are we going to get on with the issues?" But we were not in control and we learned to wait. The Assembly needed several days to get beyond jet lag and to build a common foundation of worship and Christian witness. Our Western values of efficiency and goal-oriented management were ignored. Thousands of Christians from around the world waited upon the Holy Spirit. We recognized differences, but we also began to move beyond our particularities to what we could say together out of our commitment to Jesus Christ.

I have attended a number of church meetings in my life, but never one this long. We went through the first week with energy we brought with us. By the second week we had to find sources for renewal at the meeting. Worship and Bible study took on new meaning. Relationships matured beyond the acquaintance stage. We learned to listen. And in our living together, we settled into routines that stretched to accommodate our differences. We wondered at our pluralism and yearned for a vision of how we could share something of the unity we began to know. By the time we approached the third week, however, the knowledge that we would soon leave once again highlighted our differences. In the final plenary sessions we debated questions for hours and the press tried to report the "results." But the "results" were not in resolutions and press releases. The real "results" were embedded in the fleeting Christian community we tasted somewhere between days five and fifteen. The important impact of this WCC Assembly will come from the capacity of those who were there to lead the Christian churches of the world in ways that continue to be responsible to that community.

HOW MY PRECONCEPTIONS CHANGED

The assembly was barely underway when I commented to a friend how many Indian women were present in their colorful saris. I had always thought of India as a Hindu country where only 10 percent of the people were Christian. Why were there so many delegates from India? Yet, my assumptions were limited. Ten percent of India is a lot of people. Certain Indian churches are larger than some of the leading denominations in the United States. I was embarrassed at my ignorance.

An American reporter asked a black Anglican bishop why he wanted to return to his native South Africa with its oppressive apartheid policy. He could probably "do more to help" by influencing world opinion on the outside. "You don't understand," said Bishop Tutu. "It is much easier to be a Christian in South Africa . . . there you have no doubt about what is right and what is wrong. Here it is much more difficult." I was stunned by those words. What is right and wrong? My assumptions about the good life and the Christian life have been shaped by Western democratic thinking. I began to wonder, What are the commitments and convictions that are shared by Christians in all times and places?

As the Assembly progressed I became more aware of the size and importance of Orthodox Christianity on the world scene. Because most Orthodox delegates came from Eastern Europe they were politically silent and seemingly preoccupied with liturgical theology. Yet, this large body of Christians has a spiritual legacy that is important to the whole church. I was enriched by Orthodox perspectives on worship. But I was also torn by the need to speak out about political and economic injustice in ways that could literally threaten the very existence of the World Council of Churches. In our ecumenical covenant to stay together in the WCC how much do we leave unsaid or tolerate? When the internal rivalry for representation on the Central Committee of the WCC becomes hot, what do we sacrifice for the unity of Christ's church?

Some people in the ecumenical movement helped me to see that Jesus Christ and the Christian church cannot always follow the standard of equity and fairness that I tend to assume should govern the world. Speaking out may not always be the Christian response. In fact, Christianity is not always fair or consistent. Its integrity is grounded in the Bible.

At the same time I was moved by the plea of many Christians for peace with justice. "If you do not know what hurts me, how can you say that you love me?" I came to believe with passion that ultimately the gospel does not ask us to sacrifice our care for our neighbor to keep the peace.

Many sessions were both inspiring and disturbing. I ached with a mother who feared pregnancy on a radioactive Pacific island. I listened uncomfortably as capitalism and the economic strength of the West were condemned for their inhumanity. I prayed with everyone that God's will might be done on earth as it is in heaven.

Finally, I was repeatedly humbled by the ways in which language emphasized the complexity of Christian loyalties. In spite of the fact that simultaneous translation was available in five to seven languages, the meeting was dominated by English. English, however, is not the native language of the majority of the world's Christians. There are now more Christians in Asia and Africa than in Europe and North America.

As a consequence the Assembly focused my attention upon some perplexing patterns of linguistic oppression and distortion. Because the peoples of Asia and Africa speak so many languages and dialects, English has become their common means of communication. It has allowed them to share their theological journey. At the same time this tool has the power to diminish the most creative and original aspect of Asian and African theology: its sensitivity to indigenous cultures. Christians in these "younger churches" must constantly work to protect themselves from the "Western" myths and values that are implied with the use of "Western" languages.

On the other hand, for those of us from North America or western Europe who are native speakers of English or French or German there is a different problem. The dominance of "our" language at the Assembly reinforces the misconception that Christianity can be equated with "Western" cultural values. We are called to separate Christ and culture.

At Vancouver I learned that every Christian is by definition bicultural. Christians in all places are challenged to combine their faith and their cultural context in creative ways. Those of us rooted in "Western" Christian history and those of us who are native speakers of English must take care not to dominate the conversation. Although it is easy to become impatient with broken phrases and strange syntax, we need to listen. As American Christians we are called to examine our culture-bound perspectives *and* we are invited to open ourselves to the Christian witness and potential of the two-thirds world.

REFLECTING OUT OF MY EXPERIENCE

The experience of Vancouver reshaped my theology and tested my faith in many ways. I returned home changed. I told everyone all about the programs and I showed them my pictures, but the deeper impact of this experience upon my faith will continue for many years. As a result of Vancouver my horizons are different. I am standing on new ground and I am seeing things that I have never seen.

First of all, *I am standing with some people I did not stand with before I went to Vancouver.* In the months that followed I kept meeting other people with similar experiences. One Sunday evening I was asked to speak to a very conservative church near San Francisco about the ecumenical movement. The congregation was notorious for its antagonism toward the WCC and the National Council of Churches. For years it had refused to give any monies to ecumenical ventures. I prepared myself with answers to the predictable questions about political entanglements and Communist leanings. I was ready for the worst.

But I was in for a surprise. The pastor of that church had also gone to Vancouver "to see for himself" and to document firsthand the dangers of the WCC. He had his biases and he was highly critical of much that he saw. But he also confessed that the Christians he had met in Vancouver had changed his thinking about the church and the ecumenical movement. He had talked with Christian socialists who shared facts and figures that highlighted the problems created by multinational corporations in their lands. He had listened to biblically informed leaders call for social justice programs without compromising their evangelical faith. He had been unable to fault the piety and honesty of Christian leaders when they refused to align themselves with either Communism or capitalism. By the time the evening was over this conservative evangelical pastor admitted that the easy equations between democracy, capitalism, and Christianity were not acceptable. He called his congregation to rethink its parochial and isolationist position.

Politically and theologically I was (and I still am) very different from that pastor. But in the afterglow of Vancouver we shared a common horizon, and out of that experience we were able to hear each other in new ways and appreciate some new insights. The global reality of the Christian church we encountered at Vancouver stretched our understandings of theology, the church, and the place of the Bible in our faith.

Furthermore, even as I grew more aware that Christians need to and can change, I also gained an appreciation for the strength of American values that persist in spite of change. In American religious history Christians have worked successfully to protect the faith and the church from too much change. American Christians have believed that religion should go deeper than personal opinion or passing fad. One observer of American popular culture notes that the "grass-roots mind changes at a glacial tempo."

> It survives the rise and fall of idea systems, of doomsday forecasters, of charismatic personalities, of each new alienated generation, and of technological revolutions. . . . It loves novelty, but wisely rejects it as a way of life. The story of the grass-roots mind is a tale of basic composure in the face of the wrenching influences of the twentieth century.[2]

Generally speaking, this composure has been a strength. It has protected Christianity from fads. It has given people confidence to risk. It has rooted the biblical faith in the daily routine. In reflecting upon my Vancouver experience I have a new appreciation for the grass-roots mind. I know that it is important to ground my Christian conviction in the particular realities of my people, even as I have new confidence in the capacity of Christian people to change.

In the second place, *as a result of Vancouver I now live out my faith with some new insights.* Attitudes that were once unexamined have been refined. For example, I have changed my naive assumption that life in America is better than life in most other places of the world. Even though I am not always proud of my country, before Vancouver I tended to think that most Christians would choose to live in America or Western Europe, if they could. I discovered, however, that many Christians do not have these desires. The majority of the world's Christians resent American imperialistic attitudes. They see great ambiguity and even evil in America. They may use the English language as a tool for communication with other Christians, but they do not appreciate or cling to its cultural legacy.

Against this critique I can now see my culture more honestly. America has its faults, but it also has its strengths. We must take care not to equate our faith with political and economic ideologies. But, we must also share the human freedoms we uphold. America has made some mistakes, but it also carries important global responsibilities. There are important interconnections between the Christian faith and the political order.

Also, as a "typical Yankee" my approach to Vancouver was predominantly intellectual and verbal. Before going, I read the issue papers and I prepared my mind for the challenge. I went to the Assembly eager to learn, to be informed intellectually. When things did not flow logically, or keep moving, I became impatient.

I discovered, however, that even this approach was culture-bound. Americans are goal-oriented rationalists. We want to debate the issues and produce resolutions. We are ready to argue about issues. Our response is invariably colored by the belief that the United States has global responsibilities. Yet, I came to realize that this bias actually cultivates a narrow neighborhood mentality about the world. Instead of being equally open to all options, we usually include others only as part of "our backyard."

Non-American delegates and visitors to Vancouver do not approach the world this way. They refuse to see things through American glasses. They look at the whole picture and sometimes share insights virtually unavailable to me.

Furthermore, the way they worked at Vancouver was as important as what they produced. The majority of delegates were concerned about worship, music, and the amount of free time they had to share a cup of tea and cultivate new friendships. They refused to be rushed. They patiently endured the verbiage. Bible study, prayer, and pictures were more important than resolutions. They reminded me over and over again that God's world includes many things that Americans usually ignore.

Since returning home I have a greater appreciation for the Bible and its capacity to shape faith communities in our complex world. Most Americans do not understand how Christianity influences society. We find it difficult to use our faith to criticize our culture.

In the churches of the two-thirds world, however, the Bible is an important critical tool. To be a Christian is to be bicultural. When Christians participate in the new faith community of the church they reshape cultures. They translate the meaning of the gospel of Jesus Christ into fitting faith and practice for each contemporary setting.

One of the few things all Christians have in common is the Bible. The historical and theological patterns of Western civilization do not always communicate effectively to Christians in Africa and Asia. Established liturgical and ecclesiastical habits produce problems. But when these "younger" Christians embrace the gospel of Jesus Christ and study the Bible to learn God's will for today, the transforming power of Christianity becomes evident. I am convinced that only when Christians study the Bible together will we find our oneness in Christ.

Since my experience at Vancouver I am more appreciative of other cultures, nonverbal communication, and the importance of the Bible. As a theological educator I have also become more interested in questions of evangelism and mission.

In the past, "first world" educational missionaries have taken "Western" understandings of Christianity to every part of the globe. Christianity has sought to raise up indigenous leadership to minister to the needs of the world's peoples. Yet, in most cases education has followed "Western" patterns.

At Vancouver I experienced this as a benefit and a problem. On the one hand, because there are common educational assumptions held by many leaders of churches in different parts of the world,

Christian educational mission work has facilitated ecumenical dialogue. The World Council of Churches itself depends upon the common educational history of its leadership. On the other hand, because these educational values are often "Westernized," I know that many Asian and African Christians have a difficult time dealing with biblical and theological material on their own terms.

If theological education is to create a global context for empowering ministry throughout the entire world it needs to explore new ways of helping "third world" churches grow in theological insight. Listening more carefully to the needs and affirmations of the so-called uneducated would be a good beginning.

Third, and finally, *Vancouver has changed my theology and influenced the ways in which I understand my faith in the world.* Certain horizons once hidden by trees, or covered with clouds, have now come into view.

I am newly aware, as I seek to share the importance of my Vancouver experience, of how difficult it is for people to value religion in the North American context. Indeed, we live in a society where religion does not have the central importance and power it once enjoyed. People may still attend church and speak generally about God and country, but theological seriousness is rare. The Christian religiosity that dominated American history for over two hundred years no longer exists. We live in a secular society. Today, the so-called mainline churches are far from the center of power. In fact, being a Christian in America has become "marginal."

This new reality changes my understanding of theology, biblical study, and the ecumenical movement. It means that I have a great deal in common with my Christian sisters and brothers around the world. As a member of the worldwide "marginal" faith community I am increasingly able to appreciate and more eager to seek ecumenical support.

At the same time I have also become less tolerant of the rampant individualism and narcissism of contemporary American society. Human freedom is not an end unto itself. Faith is not an isolated personal decision for Christ or an individual spiritual journey. I do not believe that Christians can live in isolation.

In spite of increasing marginality it appears that Christians need wider and wider communities of support for worship and mission.

Living out a commitment to the Christian gospel today calls for serious efforts at communal and shared endeavors. The church of Jesus Christ is a worldwide Christian community working for peace through its commitment to individual and corporate justice. And all steps toward Christian unity that seek to heal the divisions wrought by past wars and historical tensions cannot be ignored.

Even my understanding of the theme of the WCC Assembly, "Jesus Christ Life of the World," has been transformed by further reflection upon my Vancouver experiences. Before Vancouver I viewed the theme with naive Christian confidence. Jesus Christ was the "global glue" that would support Christians in a secular world. In that name Christians were united. I was a bit uneasy with the judgment implied upon peoples of other faiths, but I celebrated the fact that Christians could confess their unity in Christ.

At the Assembly, however, I discovered that there was great anger and resentment among many Asian and African Christians in reaction to so-called Christian evangelism. Missionary outreach was seen as cultural and political imperialism. I became cynical and discouraged. Well then, I thought, how can anyone say that Jesus Christ is the life of the world? American missionaries had tried to, as best they knew how, and look where it got them. Thanks and no thanks. It appeared impossible to share the faith without falling once again into the sins of oppression and colonialism. I was wary. To say that Jesus Christ was the life of the world was either meaningless or impossible.

After further reflection on my experience, however, I find that my understanding of the theme has turned itself inside out. In singing the wonderful song written by Doreen Potter, "Jesus where can we find you, in our world today?" I came to realize that to confess "Jesus Christ Life of the World" is not saying to the world, We have something you don't have, come and be like us; rather, we are saying, God in Christ has already redeemed the world and we see that life in Jesus Christ. The task is not to take Jesus Christ to the world, the task is to discover the reality of Christ already in the world . . . in creation, in life and death, in brokenness and in healing. To put it very colloquially, instead of being the "haves," with something for the "have-nots," I now realize that the confession of "Jesus Christ Life of the World" is a confession that we have already "been had."

My theological horizon has shifted. I am now standing in a new place. The horizon is no longer between those who know and love Christ and those who do not. The horizon is between God and all of the earth's peoples. To confess that Jesus Christ is the life of the world is to stretch one's knowledge of life and of the world.[3]

FAITH IN A CHANGED CONTEXT

Through my experiences at Vancouver I came to a new conscious-ness of myself as a Christian and a North American. As a result I have changed the way in which I interpret my place in the world. Furthermore, I now look with new appreciation and concern at other cultures, nonverbal communication, Bible study, and theo-logical education. My sense of solidarity with Christians in other parts of the world has been enhanced, even though I realize that European and North American perspectives no longer inform the. majority of the world's Christians. Out of this experience I have learned in a very personal way what it means to be marginal and that American Christianity is marginal. I have also accepted my need for community. Finally, I have reinterpreted the theological affirmation "Jesus Christ Life of the World" so that it expresses my experience of God's universal love.

I believe, however, that one does not have to go to Vancouver to discover new horizons. In our fast-moving society Americans need only become aware of change to explore new contexts for their faith. By asking, What is happening? How is it changing us? and How does change impinge upon our faith? we will discover new insights into our society, church, and theology. We may still be at "home," but it will not be the same place. By expanding our horizons we will discern more clearly exactly where we stand.

NOTES

1. Preparatory materials for the Sixth Assembly of the World Council of Churches in Vancouver include: *Images of Life: An Invitation to Bible Study. Prepared for the Sixth Assembly of the WCC* (Geneva: World Council of Churches, 1982); "Issue Papers," prepared for Sixth Assembly of the WCC, 1982; John Poulton, *The Feast of Life: A Theological Reflection on the Theme "Jesus Christ Life of the World"* (Geneva: World Coun-

CHANGING CONTEXTS OF OUR FAITH

cil of Churches, 1982); "Toward Vancouver, 1983," the entire issue of *Mid-Stream* 21 (October 1982).

Reports on the assembly include: "Ecumenism among the North American Churches and Societies," the entire issue of *Mid-Stream* 22 (July–October 1983); Gill, David, ed., *Gathered for Life: Official Report VI Assembly of the World Council of Churches* (Grand Rapids: Wm. B. Eerdmans; Geneva: World Council of Churches, 1983).

All materials on the WCC can be ordered from the WCC, 475 Riverside Dr., New York, NY 10115.

2. Conal Furay, *The Grass-Roots Mind in America: The American Sense of Absolutes* (New York: Franklin Watts, 1977), 16–17.

3. See Barbara Brown Zikmund, "As Disturbing Promise," in *Discovering the Church* (Philadelphia: Westminster Press, 1983), 89–106.

3
RETELLING THE STORY

Reinterpreting the Biblical   **KATHLEEN FARMER**
Tradition as a Woman

RECOLLECTIONS

It was Sunday morning, about halfway through the worship service. The sun shone through the stained glass windows, throwing patterns of light across the pews. My husband and I stood with our daughter between us, helping us hold the hymnal. She was pretending she could read all the words on the page. Then as we finished singing "God Send Us Men," my daughter stretched up to whisper in my ear, "Doesn't God send women, too?"

I almost gave her the answer I had always been given. "'Men' is a word that means us, too," my mother used to say. I had accepted that rule when I was a child. And as an English major in college I had been thoroughly drilled in "proper usage." I had learned to "include myself in" when the language I read and heard apparently left me out. But now, I suddenly realized, I could not honestly respond to my daughter in such a way! My mother's answer had sufficed for me in my youth. Why couldn't I merely hand on my mother's words to my own child? Why did I now find those words inadequate?

I remembered another warm day in a distant classroom well over a decade ago. I was in seminary, preparing myself to work as a director of Christian education in the United Methodist Church. I was the only woman among the ten or twelve students in this particular class. It was a subject in which I excelled and I had a high regard for the professor's sensitive treatment of the material. The class met for several hours at a time, with a period for a coffee break in the middle. That day, as we stood chatting in the hallway after our break, the professor called us to order, saying, "Well, gentlemen, shall we get back to work?" I can still remember the flush of anger, and the stab of rejection I felt at the time. I said, "Dr.————, don't you want me to come back, too?"

And I remembered the time I had found my daughter's building blocks pushed away in a corner under her bed. She had played happily with those blocks for several years. The box showed children building elaborate structures with the brightly colored pieces, and trying to outdo the children on the box had once been her favorite pastime. At first I put the blocks back on her toy shelf without giving the incident much thought. But the second time I had found the blocks shoved beneath the bed I had asked her, "Don't you want to play with your blocks anymore?" Giving the box a kick she had said, "I can't play with those blocks. There aren't any girls on the outside of that box!"

REFLECTIONS

The pictures on the outside of a box of toys help us decide whether or not the contents are intended for us to use. And the words a speaker uses help us decide whether or not the content of the message is meant for us to hear. The toymakers had not pictured the possibility that a small girl might enjoy building elaborate structures with their product. My daughter had recognized their opinion reflected on the box. And in spite of the fact that she had personally experienced joy and satisfaction in playing with these materials, she had allowed the manufacturers' opinion to overshadow her pleasure. She had resented it, but she had given in to their view of reality when she had thrust these toys away beneath the bed.

When my professor had used the term "gentlemen" to refer to the class of which I was a part, he had painted a mental picture for me of a group from which I was totally excluded. I could not believe he had intentionally done so. And he had not. My question had caused him to blush and he had apologized for his inappropriate choice of words. Few women had taken his courses in previous years and he had developed a habit of speaking and thinking of students as males. His experiences had shaped his speech patterns. But now his audience had changed. And those habits of speech which had stood him in good stead for many years no longer communicated his intentions to all of his listeners. We human beings use words to help us picture reality in our minds. But in speaking and listening there are two distinct sides of this picturing process. On the one hand, there is the picture the speaker *intends* to convey, and on the other hand there is the picture that the listener *actually receives* from the words that are used.

As I pondered my daughter's question "Doesn't God send women, too?" I thought not only about the author's original intentions, but also about the image that the author's words would call up in the minds of those who used his words in worship. So first of all, I wondered, when "God Send Us Men" was written or when it was sung in congregations across the nation, did those who used the word "men" really have women in mind as well? Did they really think God might, in answer to their prayers, send a woman "alert and quick," God's "lofty precepts to translate/Until the laws of Christ became/The laws and habits of the state"? and secondly, I wondered, when my daughter and other girls or women heard these words, could they picture the possibility that they themselves might be sent by God to accomplish such a task?

One of the problems we all confront as we try to communicate with each other stems from the fluid nature of human language. In a living language, words often change their meanings over a relatively brief period of time. Not long ago the National Council of Teachers of English acknowledged that in current English usage the masculine pronouns and such terms as man, men, brother, brotherhood, and so forth had begun to lose the generic sense they carried in older usage. So for an ever-increasing number of listeners today, the term "men" would not call up a mental image of both male and female human beings. And yet, I reflected, the words we used in our faith traditions to talk about God and about ourselves, the words we used to describe God's actions and our responses, would still function very much like the pictures on the outside of a box of toys. Such words and pictures would continue to tell the listeners whether or not they had a place in the reality the words represent. What would the words we presently use communicate to the children of the future? Would the girls of my daughter's generation decide that the hymns and prayers and other traditional expressions of the church's faith had left them out of the picture? Would they feel the need to shove those traditions away "under the bed" when they discovered that they were not reflected in the "picture" on the church's box? Or would we, their elders in the faith, learn to retell "the old, old story" in new ways, using words that clearly include all of God's children in the picture?

Up to this point in my reflections I had been assuming that my daughter's question was primarily a question of language and communication. But suppose the author of "God Send Us Men" had clearly intended the word "men" in these lines to mean only male human beings? If that were the case "Doesn't God send women, too?" would become a question about *God's* intentions. Perhaps I had misunderstood the point of the question. Maybe my child simply wanted to be reassured—to hear me state plainly that I did indeed believe that in spite of what the hymn said, God intended for both women and men to take an active role in the working out of God's will in the world. Or then again, she may have been wondering whether some day in the future she herself might be one of those sent by God to help "translate lofty precepts" into the "laws and habits of the state." If so, I needed to consider what I could do to help her discover where she fit into God's plans. Her dilemma was not unlike the one I had faced when I had decided to go to seminary.

The church had always played an important part in my life. It was there I felt consistently affirmed as a child of God. But my feeling of being called by God into full-time Christian service resembled the gentle, steady pull of a lazy river current more than it did a whirlwind or a burning bush experience. All through high school and college I had resisted this gentle but persistent "pull." But when I had suddenly decided to enroll in seminary, I had felt a release of tension, such as moving with rather than against a current brings. As I delved into theological studies I felt a deepening sense of rightness in my choice of vocation. This was where I belonged! This was where I fit. This was what God wanted me to be doing!

Imagine my surprise when I first discovered that there were many people in the church, even some from my own home town, who disapproved on biblical grounds of my decision to get a seminary degree. They quoted 1 Cor. 14:34–36 ("Women should keep silence in the churches") and 1 Tim. 2:11–15 ("Permit no woman to teach or to have authority over men") as evidence that I had misunderstood my calling. What a dilemma this posed for me! How was I to weigh the authority of such texts over against the experiences I had had of being drawn by God into this field of study? Furthermore, how could I reconcile either 1 Cor. 14:34–36 or 1 Tim. 2:11–15 with what Paul said in Gal. 3:27–28 ("For as many of you as were baptized into Christ have put on Christ. There is neither Jew nor Greek, there is neither slave nor free, there is neither male nor female, for you are all one in Christ Jesus")? In 1 Corinthians 11 women are told they should be veiled when praying or prophesying in public but in 1 Cor. 14:34 they are told to be silent altogether. Had Paul changed his mind over the course of his career? How did his rabbinic background affect his ideas of what was proper? How did Paul's statement compare with the story about what Jesus said to Mary and Martha in Luke 10:38–42? (When Martha wanted her sister Mary to assume the traditional serving role of a woman in the society of their time, Jesus rebuked her and affirmed Mary's right to "sit at the Lord's feet" and to listen to his teachings as his other disciples did.) Where did women such as Deborah (who was a prophet, a judge, and a military leader in Israel) fit into God's overall scheme?

Ironically, it was those who opposed my choice of vocation on biblical grounds who actually lured me deeper and deeper into biblical studies. I soon discovered that there were passages in the Bible that could be used to support either side of almost any controversial issue. In the nineteenth century, biblical texts had been used by Christians to argue both for and against slavery as an institution in our society. In more recent times, sincere Christians had used the Bible to support both pacifist or nonresistant positions and positions supporting or allowing Christians to participate in war. The Scriptures certainly contained passages that seemed to reduce women to the level of property, belonging to men as did slaves and cattle. But there were also many passages in which women were seen to act as responsible persons in their own right, accepting positions of leadership and authority in both social and religious institutions. In fact, I was surprised to find how many women there were whose stories were totally new to me, whose roles had never been highlighted in my church school materials, and whose acts of faith had never been the subject of any sermons I had heard.

Even texts that traditionally had been used against women I found were open to other, quite reasonable interpretations. For instance, the story in Gen. 2:18–25 says (according to the King James Version) that God created woman as a *help meet* for the man. Many people who read those two words assumed that "help" implied inferiority and they forgot that in King James' time "meet" was a word that meant "suitable." Few bothered to investigate the Hebrew word used for "help," but if they had they would have found that the word is often used in the Old Testament to refer to the Lord (as in Ps. 33:20; 70:5; 115:9, 10, 11) and has no sense of inferior status attached to it at all. Similarly, the English word "meet" in the King James Version translates a Hebrew term meaning "corresponding to" or "appropriate." There is little reason to believe that this story in Gen. 2:18–25 was intended to justify the subordination of all women to all men for all time. Even when Paul comments on this passage in 1 Cor. 11:3 the word he uses, which is translated "head," means "source" or "origin" and does *not* contain the idea of one person "ruling" over another.

I discovered that the very same evidence in Scripture had been used by different interpreters to support completely different conclusions. For instance, interpreters could not agree on the significance of the veil women were told to use when praying or prophesying in public. Some thought it signified submission or subordination, while others saw it as a sign of authority that gave women the freedom to participate freely in worship. Or, to give another example, I found that in discussing Genesis 2, interpreters on both sides of the question of women's God-intended status noted that the male human being is said to have been created first and the female second. Some see this as an argument for male superiority—assuming what is created first is superior to subsequent efforts. But others argue that in Genesis 1 human beings are said to have been created last, coming after all of the other creatures, as the culmination of creation. Thus, they conclude, being created last does not at all imply inferiority.

Some interpreters argued that females had a "derivative" origin—being made from the "original" male. But others noted that man was said to have been made from earth and since this was never taken to mean that men were inferior to the substance from which they were made, there was no reason to assume that women were inferior to the substance from which they were made. In Gen. 1:26–27 the Hebrew term *adam* (translated "man") has a plural generic sense meaning "humankind" or humanity in general. In verse 26 ("God said, 'let us make *adam* in our image, after our likeness; and let *them* have dominion . . .'") dominion is given to *them* in the plural. In verse 27 the image of God is specified as containing both male and female halves of humanity ("God created humankind in his image . . . male and female he created them"). Some interpreters argued that his concept of humanity is the governing idea under which should fall all subsequent passages referring to women's status in God's intentions for creation. Others thought this statement's importance was greatly diminished by the emphasis Paul put on the stories that followed in Genesis 2—3.

For every text that could be used to argue for the inferiority of women there was another that could be used as evidence that God intended for women and men to be equal and interdependent partners acting as God's "images" (or representatives) in the world. Those who argued that human disobedience (in Genesis 3) had negated the created order and that the subordination of women was ordained by God as a continuing punishment were countered by those who argued that Christ brought redemption that changed the old, sinful order and renewed the full partnership of male and female in creation. Some were convinced that Paul was laying down a universal commandment in 1 Cor. 14:34, prohibiting all women everywhere from teaching or ruling over men. Others saw his comments applying only to the community to which the letter was addressed, a community influenced by Greek mystery cults in which women were dominant figures, and in which the term translated "speak" referred to "talking nonsensically" such as was done in the speaking-in-tongues of the mystery cults.

I dealt with the biblical texts dealing specifically with women, expecting to find in them some clear-cut guidelines concerning my role in carrying out God's work in the world. What I had found was a wide variety of apparently conflicting opinions concerning God's intentions for women's lives. One thing soon became inescapably clear: there were no neutral ways of reading any of these controversial texts. Every reader came to a text with previous experiences and with some expectations concerning what she or he would find within it. All interpreters' conclusions were colored to some extent or another by their expectations, whether they consciously recognized it or not! Whether we are reading a newspaper, a novel, a poem, or a biblical text, we all call upon past experience to understand what we are reading. All interpretation, whether it is of a biblical text or not, involves a mental "pacing" back and forth between what we already know (from our past experiences) and what we are trying to discover (the meaning of the text at hand). We do this rather automatically, without thinking about the process, until someone questions our conclusions.

I only began to look at my own (subconscious) assumptions about the Bible when I found that others understood the same texts differently than I did. For instance, I had always assumed that most of the people whose stories were preserved in Scripture were admirable characters. I expected biblical characters to act in praiseworthy ways, for the most part. I thought that I could use most of them as models for my own behavior. Of course there were some exceptions. Judas had betrayed our Lord. It seemed clear that this was not praiseworthy behavior! But Peter, who was in many ways an admirable character, had also denied knowing Jesus at a crucial time. Abraham had received praise for his faithful response to the Lord's call. But was his attempt to shield himself from harm by passing his wife off as his sister (Genesis 12) equally worthy of praise? There were stories of women who apparently acted admirably and efficiently in leadership roles (Shiphrah and Puah in Exod. 1:15–21, Deborah, Ruth, Esther, the unnamed woman described in Prov. 31:10–31, Lydia in Acts 16, Phoebe in Romans 16, Mary Magdalene and the other Mary at Jesus' tomb in Matthew 28 and Luke 24, etc.). But there were others whose actions were more difficult to judge (such as the deception urged by Jacob's mother Rebekah and practiced by his wife Rachel).

In a few cases there were clues within the story itself to indicate how the narrator evaluated the action being described. Sometimes the consequences of a person's behavior were unfavorable. But in others, favorable results appeared to follow quite deplorable deeds. What may have appeared to me to be reprehensible behavior did not often have clearly unfavorable consequences. For instance, Jacob tricked his blind old father in order to defraud his brother in Genesis 27. And yet, as he ran away from his brother's anger, Jacob was given the promise of God's continuing presence and blessing (in Genesis 28). Other stories describe how Lot's daughters committed incest with their father in order to have children of their own (in Gen. 19:30–38) and how Tamar passed herself off as a prostitute in order to get Judah to father her sons (in Genesis 38). And yet, the children produced by these women were also said to have become the ancestors of the Davidic line to which Jesus' own ancestry is traced! In by far the majority of cases, the biblical texts themselves merely *describe* (and do not either approve or condemn) the actions of these human figures whose stories have been handed down to us through the centuries.

I found that each of us had to decide for ourselves whether a particular action described in the Bible was an instance of faith or of unfaith, an example of strength or of weakness, of right or wrong. I had to judge what I read according to standards drawn from somewhere *other* than the particular text I was trying to understand. What kind of scales could I use to weigh the intentions of specific passages? Some people suggested that an interpreter had to look to the Bible overall in order to recognize what the gospel was all about. One needed to find basic themes or central, dominant teachings that could be used as a sort of yardstick for measuring specific texts. In other words, if I wanted to find out what God's intentions were for women, I needed to ask what the basic concerns of God appeared to be as they emerged from an overall reading of both the Old and the New Testament, rather than focusing solely upon texts that specifically mentioned women. What are the dominant themes in Jesus' teaching? What are the essential points of the Gospel? What picture does the entire body of Scriptures give me about the nature of God, the nature of humankind, or the nature of the relationship between them? Answers to each of these questions could very well function as criteria with which to judge what one's attitude toward any specific passage ought to be. Thus a responsible interpreter would use the wide variety of texts available to build a composite picture. And this picture would then in turn be used to weigh the respective merits of specific texts.

The problem that continued to plague me for many years was *how* to explain the variety I had found within Scripture. I needed a model that would allow me to understand the ambiguities, the inconsistencies, and the differences of opinion—but a model that would still allow me to see how the Scriptures played a distinctive and irreplaceable role in helping me understand what God is like and what God wants of humankind. It finally occurred to me that my own tradition offered a key to this puzzle. In the "doctrinal guidelines" of the 1980 edition of *The Book of Discipline of the United Methodist Church*, I found the Bible referred to as "the deposit of a unique testimony to God's self-disclosure," and as "the constitutive witness to God's self-revelation."[1]

I began to consider how it was that *I* revealed myself to someone else. How does one person reveal herself to another? How do others come to know what I am like? How do they learn what I value most highly or what I expect of myself and of those around me? If several persons who knew me well but who had experienced me in different ways (as a student, as a teacher, or a sister, or a daughter, or a mother, and so on) were to describe me to someone else, would their understandings of who I am, what I expect of them or what they can expect of me correspond exactly? Would this process of self-revelation take place all at once, or would it happen gradually over a long period of acquaintance? If God had revealed God's Self over a long period of Israel's history to different people, living in quite different cultural, political, and historical or personal settings, then it ought to come as no surprise to us to find that these different witnesses had sometimes perceived their relationships to God in different ways. Those who "trampled upon the needy," who "bought the poor for silver and the needy for a pair of sandals" (Amos 8:4–6) must surely have experienced the reality of God differently than did those who learned "to do good, seek justice, correct oppression; defend the orphan, plead for the widow" (Isa. 1:17). Because their experiences in life differed, their descriptions of God's character, God's purposes, and God's expectations did not always coincide. If we approached the Scriptures expecting to find a "deposit" of testimony in which real human beings have described how they perceived God working in their very normal human lives, we would not be dismayed to find that those witnesses sometimes disagreed with each other. It was not God's nature or God's intentions toward humankind that had changed. Rather, it was the vantage points from which the various viewers perceived the reality of God that had changed.

The Bible is also referred to in many traditions as the "Word of God." As I studied the biblical languages I discovered that the Hebrew term *dabar* means both "word" in the English sense of a verbal communication *and* something more. In the language of the Old Testament *dabar* refers to actions and events, as well as the reasons behind them. Thus the term Word of God (with a capital *W*) refers to the actions and intentions of God as they were acted out in the history of humankind. The human beings who recognized God's activity in the world described what they saw using human words (with a small *w* in the more limited sense of verbal communications).

Furthermore, these ancient witnesses used many different forms of verbal communication (poems and prose, narratives, songs, sermons, prayers, parables, chronicles, letters, proverbs, and many more) as they tried to express their understandings of God's nature and purposes in terms that their contemporaries could understand. Each individual witness used terms and concepts that were familiar to the people of the speaker's own time. It is quite clear to the careful reader that in the world in which the written forms of the Bible developed, most of the social, economic, and political power was wielded by men. Most of the poets, the historians, the religious leaders, the storytellers (and so forth) were men. In such a "patriarchal" world most of the stories told and preserved would naturally have had male protagonists. I ought not to have been surprised to find that this body of writings primarily reflected the male in that society's point of view.

The question nonetheless remained for myself and for many women whether or not such culturally and sexually biased viewpoints could have something authoritative to say to us today about who God is and who we are as women and men in relationship to God and to each other. I found that a recent generation of interpreters (often, but not always, women) had begun to comb the biblical texts for "lost," forgotten, or neglected passages that reflected the female dimensions of humankind's experiences with God. One influential scholar used the parable of the lost coin in Luke 15:8 to describe this search:

> Throughout the centuries, interpreters of scripture have explored the male language of faith, full and overflowing. Yet the Bible itself proclaims another dimension that faith has lost—female imagery and

motifs. Much as the ancient housekeeper of the New Testament, while possessing nine coins, searched for the tenth which she had lost, so we too, while acknowledging the dominance of male language in scripture, have lit a lamp, swept the house, and sought diligently for that which was lost.[2]

Given the male-dominated nature of the societies that transmitted and preserved as well as recorded the Scriptures, the search for this "lost coin" has been remarkably successful. The Scriptures themselves contain feminine images (or metaphors) of God which have been shaded over by centuries of neglect (e.g., God conceiving a people, writhing in labor pains, bringing forth a child, nursing it, and grieving over its disobedience and death, or God gathering people together as a mother hen gathers her brood under her wings). These ancient witnesses also preserved stories in which we have only recently begun to notice that "the brave and bold decisions of women embody and bring to pass the blessings of God."[3]

However, even the most optimistic interpreters had to admit that the recoverable remnant of material reflecting women's experiences of God in Scripture was but a small percentage of the whole. And in recent years an increasing number of women have questioned whether being able to recover one lost coin among ten is enough to justify their using this material as an ultimate authority for living out their lives in faith. As one woman defined the problem, "We are faced with the issues of how a pervasively patriarchal document can continue to communicate anything of value to those who reject all such oppression."[4]

What kind of authority did this "deposit of testimony" we called the Bible have over me? What kind of authority would it have for my daughter in years to come?

RETELLING

It was a child's question that had prompted my reflections. My daughter's question had made me realize how my expectations had changed over a period of years. I no longer expected the Bible to function like an advice column in the newspaper or like a book of rules in the "game" of life. I no longer expected this collection of ancient records to provide me with a stockpile of ready-made answers for every question. I still believed it had something uniquely true to say to me about reality—about human reality (what humans are like) and about divine reality (what God is like). I no longer hoped to be able to separate the Word of God from the little, individual, human words that convey each speaker's glimpse of the reality of God to us today. But I still believed that the reality of God's nature continually managed to escape the limits put upon it by those who had recorded their perceptions of it in human terms. I wanted to find a way to pass on to my daughter a picture of our traditions that would allow her to recognize its plurality and rejoice in its variety without being frightened by its inconsistencies, its ambiguities, or its human limitations.

I decided to begin by teaching her the story of the six blind people who went to discover for themselves what an elephant was like. One fell against the animal's side and concluded that the elephant was very like a wall. Another, encountering a pointed tusk, declared it clear that the elephant was very like a spear. The one who encountered the elephant's ear was confirmed in the belief that the elephant was like a leaf, and so forth. Each person, standing in a different place, had experienced something different. Each had seized upon a part of the truth about the reality they were experiencing (i.e., the elephant). Of course we human beings cannot reach out and touch God in quite the same way. And when it comes to "seeing" God, we too are blind. But each person who wants to find out what God is like can find out a part of the truth about God by reaching out from where she stands in life. But we have to remember that what seems to be truth from where we stand cannot be the whole truth about God.

The Bible is an extremely good place to go to find out how many, many different people over thousands of years of history have reached out and discovered part of the truth of God—whatever parts could be seen or felt from their particular viewpoints in life. The stories in the Bible are about human beings who were very similar to us in many ways. Sometimes they were faithful and sometimes they were faithless, but in every case, their stories show us that God found ways of using them all, even in the midst of their faithlessness, to carry out God's will in the world. So the Bible tells us better than any other book anywhere about what many people "saw" when they looked for God and how they acted (sometimes good and sometimes bad) both while they were searching for God and after they had found out what God was like for them. I think the way God has chosen to let these different witnesses speak for themselves, in spite of their faults, or their weaknesses, or their "blindness," indicates that God wants us to learn to think for ourselves, based on what we can see from where we stand, about who God is and what God is doing in the world around us.

You remember when you decided not to play with those blocks anymore after you saw there weren't any girls on the box? Well, you will probably find out eventually that some people don't think girls should grow up to be ministers or leaders in the church. Some people don't think women should have equal responsibilities with men in carrying out God's work in the world. But you know that your best friend's mother is a pastor, preaching and teaching in a church of her own. And you know that I work in a seminary, teaching future ministers about their traditions.

We have felt ourselves to be in equal partnership with men in God's eyes. We believe God needs and wants both women and men to work together to carry out God's plans in the world. Some people may tell you that you don't belong in the picture. But when it comes to looking for what God wants, you are the one to decide. You can't let anyone else do your looking for you.

That is what I told my daughter: I believe God sends women, too. And God may have plans for you!

What would you have done if you were in my place?

NOTES

1. *The Book of Discipline of the United Methodist Church* (Nashville: United Methodist Church, 1980), 78–79.

2. Phyllis Trible, *God and the Rhetoric of Sexuality* (Philadelphia: Fortress Press, 1978), 200.

3. Ibid., 195. Trible here comments on Ruth.

4. Mary Ann Tolbert, "Defining the Problem: The Bible and Feminist Hermeneutics," *Semeia* 28 (1983): 125.

4

TRANSFORMING SUFFERING

Struggling with Life as
an Asian American

ROY I. SANO

RECOLLECTIONS

It seemed like an innocent request, but proved life-changing. I was attending the international Consultation on Minority Issues and Mission Strategies, May 1974, in Kyoto, Japan. The Rev. Charles Chung-Ryul Song asked me to deliver an envelope to his friend from South Korea who was also participating. When Rev. Song turned over the envelope to me he gave specific instructions: "When you deliver this envelope to Rev. Kim Kwan-Suk, make sure no one else is around. Only speak to him briefly." I had some inkling of the reasons behind these instructions even if they sounded a bit melodramatic.

When I turned over the envelope to Rev. Kim in Japan, he insisted I visit Korea while I was in Asia. Arrangements were hastily made through him and Rev. Song. I was hosted in Seoul, Korea by a husband and wife team who were intensely involved in the efforts to democratize that nation. The husband, Dr. Chung Yil-Hyung, had the longest tenure in the National Assembly of any representative; the wife, Dr. Lee Tae-Young, was the first woman lawyer in that nation and the founder of an internationally recognized family life counseling center. Through them I met several key figures in the movement for human rights who were under house arrest. They reported the costly and distorting schemes for economic development. Laborers, many of them youthful boys and girls from the countryside, worked long hours for low wages and under hazardous conditions. Many occupied cramped quarters in cities that over-looked basic human needs. The workers had little, if any, bargaining power. The leaders described the harassments, imprisonment, and torture they had suffered for their stands against the repressive measures of President Park Chung-Hee's regime. With the concern for national security so dominant and pervasive, the president turned their country into a prison of protection. No wonder they pleaded for changes in United States foreign policies which supported such tyrannies.

As I prepared to return, I was given envelopes with messages which I was told to conceal under my clothes. As I went through customs at the airport I was subjected to a body search which others in front of me had not had. An officer discovered the packages under my belt. He was excited and took the items to his superiors. I tried making a scene by protesting loudly. Waving my U.S. passport only proved to be a laughable gesture. After a momentary detention and interrogation, they finally returned the envelopes and allowed me to proceed.

When I reached Tokyo on my way home, I sent a post card notifying my hosts that the trip had gone well. I hoped the message would assure them that I had the packages and they did not need to worry. They never received the card.

Shortly after returning to Oakland, California, Rev. Song visited me. If the envelopes were safely brought home, he was to wire a contact person in New York with the following message: "My son is out of the hospital and I am relieved." If I did not succeed in bringing the packages to the U.S., he was to say, "My son is still in the hospital and I am concerned." He also said I should not answer telephone calls from persons with a Korean accent. I was to take their names and telephone numbers, and promise to return the call when I was not busy. I received five such calls. They came from various parts of the country—Los Angeles, New York, and Washington, D.C. When I checked the names with Rev. Song, as he told me I should, only two were recognized by Korean American supporters of human rights struggles in their homeland. Korean Americans were taking such precautionary measures because they had experienced the intimidating operations of the Korean Central Intelligence Agency (KCIA) long before the reputable newspapers in the U.S. reported them.

RESOURCES FOR REFLECTION

These initial experiences with human rights movements among Korean American Christians had a profound effect upon me. A decade has passed, but I still have in my office at school a picture of the husband and wife team who hosted me on my first visit to Korea. I introduce them as my "spiritual parents" for my work as a teacher at a theological seminary, my responsibilities in the church, and my involvements in the community. I recognize my indebtedness to my biological parents. I marvel at the warm Christian home they provided despite the economic difficulties and the disruptions Japanese Americans experienced in the wartime hysteria against them in the 1940s. At the same time, Dr. Chung and Dr. Lee have induced some basic transformations in my faith and calling which I try acknowledging with their portrait in my study at the school.

Since the series of testimonies in this book focuses on the changes in our reading and uses of the Bible, I will describe how the changes came about. My rereading of the Bible and the new uses I found for it fit into what I call a *spiral of action and reflection.*

By way of explanation, I found myself moving through a sequence of action, then reflection, and back to action. I say the sequence is a "spiral" because the reflection moved me from action on one plane to action that I experienced on another plane. Behavior was not only changed, but ingredients in the action were altered. A circle, as distinct from a spiral, would have simply returned me to action on the same plane, or behavior with the same qualities. What made the sequence of action-reflection-action into a spiral and not a circle was the "reflections" that were introduced to me. Speaking in general terms, two lines of reflection proved particularly crucial. In sum, a "change of consciousness" about my context occurred.

First, I recognized that I had been living with a misleading picture of the world. In carrying out routine requests, I encountered some things that I had not anticipated and my view of the world could not process. On the surface, I was delivering envelopes among old friends. What I confronted, however, were actors, events, and forces with international connections which manage societies and manipulate people. Second, having become suspicious of the picture I had of my context, I explored possible alternatives.

It was as if one were driving with a map of Kansas while traversing a treacherous pass in the Rocky Mountains. There is nothing wrong, of course, with a map of Kansas while driving through Kansas, but the straight lines and rectangular crossings we associate with a map of Kansas hardly prepare drivers for the twists and turns of roads in the Rockies. After one is frightened by a dangerous precipice at an unanticipated turn, one begins fishing for another map. Hence, "actions" that brought me up short prompted "reflections." I began questioning the adequacy of the picture of the world with which I was living; I started scrambling for an alternative. By speaking therefore of a "change of consciousness" that a line of reflection can create, I have in mind a shift in the picture of the world that locates where we are and guides our action.

Our resources for reflection were "scientific" (in the sense that one draws on a field of knowledge), biblical, and theological. Each resource contributes toward a picture of the course of events in which we are living and thus provides clues for fitting action in our situation. Before we consider these various resources for reflection, however, it may be useful to rehearse additional actions among Asian Americans that the violation of human rights prompted. These experiments will suggest something of the data that aroused reflections among us. Parallels with the experience of other people will be explored later as we consider the relevance of these experiences for the reader.

My initial experiences in May 1974 stirred deeper involvements. I found myself sharing the challenges to faithful witness and service that the Korean Christians inspired. I cited their prayer meetings where intelligence agents tape-recorded testimonies and prayers that violated strict rules against criticizing the government. I reported how participants left such meetings to face hundreds of riot police. These prayer meetings resulted in people "putting legs on their prayers." Protest marches occasionally followed these "seasons of prayer."

After a second visit to Korea with an Asian American Goodwill Visitation Team in November of 1974, actions became more concrete. We picketed the South Korean Consulate in San Francisco and protested the imprisonment of prominent leaders such as the Roman Catholic poet and playwright, Kim Chie-Ha; the woman clergy who conducted Bible study for factory workers, Cho Hwa-Soon; and the political leader, Kim Dae Jung. Many of us joined a national ecumenical network which mobilized us into efforts to influence our State Department which protected the dictatorial regime, or our military which supplied the backup and training for repressive measures. Eventually international linkages were formed in efforts toward humanizing the unequal economic and social development in a society repressed by excessive national security measures.

In the meantime, Asian Americans were also aware of similar violations of human rights in the Philippines with the 1972 imposition of martial law. Very soon thereafter, we were staging demonstrations as a way of drawing attention to U.S. complicity in the injustices there. Those of us with U.S. citizenship were asked to enter the Philippine Consulates and deliver demands for the release of such prisoners as Fr. Edwardo de la Torre or Trinidad Hererra, the community organizer. During one such protest in the Consulate, a Filipina who was a naturalized citizen and employed as a church secretary was threatened in her native language so that English-speaking supporters could not understand. An official at the consulate said, "I do not know why you do these things. You know we can 'take care' of your relatives back home." In the week before her trial several months after she was arrested, the woman heard from relatives in the Philippines that her uncle had been found dead floating in a river. The autopsy arranged by the family determined that he had died from strangulation, not from drowning.

Still other concerns drew additional Asian Americans into the human rights struggles. One such incident occurred among the Taiwanese, or Formosans, as some prefer to be called. They opposed the inequities inflicted on them by the Nationalist Chinese who dominated the island of Taiwan where they fled in defeat from mainland China. A relative of one of the proponents for freedom in Taiwan who lived in the San Francisco Bay Area received a telephone call. His brother in Taiwan asked for a meeting in Hong Kong. After going to the prearranged location, he waited several days for his brother from Taiwan. Eventually he received another message instructing him to fly to Taipei, the capital of Taiwan. Upon his arrival there, he became suspicious and decided not to deplane until he could spot his brother. He was forceably removed from the airplane and then arrested. He was tried for treason and is now imprisoned for life. His kinfolk subsequently determined that the original telephone call came a few days after the brother in Taiwan was imprisoned himself, thus suggesting to them that the invitation was issued under duress.

The stories of Asian Americans in human rights efforts could continue. Those already cited indicate that the experiences of the author are only a sampling of widespread occurrences in the 1970s, with many of them far more costly. Readers can therefore understand why we began questioning what we understood was happening and what we were told we should be doing. Whether these understandings came from society at large or were nurtured within the church, the probing was quite serious and widespread.

The resources for reflection transformed the violations of human rights. The scientific resource helped us make sense of what was happening. The biblical and theological resources uncovered God's action in the course of international events which affected individuals, families, and societies. They also clarified our calling. By the time we moved through those phases of reflection, whatever we may have suffered was transformed into a basis for action that hallowed our lives. An Undergirding Divine Presence carried us into a promising future. An elaboration of the resources will explain what I have just said.

Scientific Resources

As indicated earlier, the word "science" is used with the root meaning in mind. Science comes from a word that means "knowledge." Hence, "scientific resource" refers to a field of knowledge. This resource for reflection came primarily from a social science called "political economy," or that field of study that describes economic developments and their consequences for distribution of power.

Reflections on our experiences made it very clear that certain figures had extraordinary powers in our context. The intelligence operatives and their activities could intimidate immigrants in the

68

U.S. who were far removed from the problems faced by relatives in ancestral lands. These *individuals* had international connections that could perform reprisals against those who questioned developments abroad or in their new home.

The intelligence agents and their network, however, were only a small part of other overarching linkages. Military alliances could back up their efforts. The intelligence and armed forces, in turn, served other interests. Well-meaning plans for economic development, as well as noble pursuits for modernizing societies and enriching cultural exchanges, needed protection against those who might disrupt or thwart these efforts. The primary culprit that concerned the U.S. and our allies abroad was, of course, the communist forces. Thus, the *institutions* that we had mandated to promote development, modernization, and cultural exchanges were protected by the armed services and intelligence networks against the subversion of legitimate, if not noble aspirations. These institutions included transnational corporations, think tanks, universities, communication media, and even religious organizations.

What we were therefore encountering in our actions were key *individuals,* enormous *institutions,* and the twin *ideologies* of "development" and "national security." The intentions were so noble, who could question them? Furthermore, who could question the feasibility of the dreams? They had worked successfully in the Marshall Plan and in the North Atlantic Treaty Organization (NATO). These postwar ventures benefited many people on both sides of the Atlantic. It was little wonder then that the same arrangements would be prompted elsewhere, such as in Asia. One could notice attempts to reproduce the same scenarios with Africa, Latin America, and the island societies wherever we could go.

What was not acknowledged in this romantic picture, however, were the negative aspects. The overwhelming majority of Asian Americans in the U.S. and their relatives living abroad were among those who bore the brunt of the cost in the unequal developments and suffered the consequences of repressive measures in the security considerations. An inequitable distribution of the benefits of developments and the imbalances in distribution of power to shape the course of the future resulted in gross injustices for them and their relatives.

These pictures of our locus in the social fabric in the U.S. and in the international exchanges, and these pictures of our place in the scenarios of development and national security, came as a rude awakening. We thought we had come to the Promised Land of the modern world. While we may have enjoyed many benefits of this society and were grateful, there were these distressing dimensions in our context that we could only overlook if we hardened our hearts to the sufferings of our own people or closed our eyes to our own personal experiences.

In summary, we were conscious of living under the domination of a "host of lords" who managed our lives and manipulated many more millions abroad. While the acculturation and assimilation of Asian Americans in this society may have produced conspicuous examples of people living *above* the "poverty line," reflections on our actions clearly demonstrated how much we operated *below* the "power line." While we may not always be blatantly oppressed and exploited, we recognized how we were outwitted and outmaneuvered as we sought to rectify what had gone wrong in the dreams for societies abroad which our successes in the Marshall Plan and the NATO ventures fostered. The "host of lords" includes key *individuals* and impressive *institutions* such as corporations, the military, and the intelligence networks. When these individuals and institutions were infused with the hallowed *ideologies* of "development" and "national security," the already awesome, overarching powers became principalities. To speak in terms of a "host of lords" and of "principalities and powers" already suggests our reflections were colored by the Bible. Indeed, just as the steps in the spiral of action-reflection-action are distinguishable but intermixed, so too the resources for reflection are intertwined though separable. Thus, I turn from the scientific resources of political economy to the resources for reflection on our actions that we found in the Bible.

Biblical Resources

Reflections with the resources of political economy gave us a picture of our locus in society and our place in the currents of events which fit our experiences. These reflections made us aware of our distorted readings of the Bible and the requisite corrections.

1. *Perspectives on the Bible.* Many of us Asian Americans had imbibed the perspective of leading biblical teachers who taught us. They proceeded with the assumption that they were not only *above* the "poverty line," but also above the "power line." By contrast, as noted earlier, we were aware that many Asian Americans may be *above* the poverty line, but we were as a group *below* the power line. That slight difference in consciousness explains basic changes in our reading of the Bible.

A plausible story explained the perspective of our teachers. The democratic revolutions from the seventeenth through the nineteenth centuries overturned the "three estates" that had dominated their ancestors—namely, the royalty, the nobility, and the clergy. Once their forebears, who were among the rising entrepreneurs and professionals, had dethroned those intermediaries between themselves and their God, they became the "captains of their souls and masters of their fate." That is, they saw themselves above the power line.

Their social and political successes were reinforced by achievements in the natural sciences and technologies. This provided additional proof that the picture of a world populated with suprahuman agencies overhead—the Devil and Satan, demons and angels—was discredited. If they wanted water, they did not dance to a rain god; they constructed reservoirs and dug canals. Thus, the social and technological successes convinced them that nothing intervened between themselves and their God.

2. *Misleading Uses of the Wrong Portions of the Bible.* With such a reading of their locus in society and their place in the human story, they gravitated to those parts of the Bible that corresponded with their situation. In the first place, this meant they were drawn to the Old Testament prophets who lived in the time of Israel's nationhood. This included Amos, Hosea, Micah, and Isaiah (especially chaps. 1–39). At that time, no foreign powers dominated them. No one was overhead, between themselves and their God. In the second place, those passages written when Israel or the early church lived under domination of foreign powers were passed over. Among the most vivid examples in this category were the apocalyptic books of Daniel and the Revelation which they turned over to social outcasts and the lunatic fringe. Third, our teachers tried to

reinterpret the remainder of the Bible in socially and scientifically acceptable terms. Since so much of the remaining portions of the Bible were written with a less conspicuous attention to the domination of the intervening "hosts of lords" or "principalities and powers," our teachers said we could disregard these "husks" of the Bible and live with the "kernel" of the Gospel.

3. *A Search for Alternatives.* All three of these moves were understandable in their social and historical setting. But they were less useful for reflections on our context. We recognized that in recent decades, a new "host of lords," a new set of "principalities and powers," emerged between ourselves and our God. One did not need to be blatantly manipulated to recognize how one is managed; one did not need to be desperately poor to recognize how powerless one can be on matters that are crucial to principalities and powers. Working for the welfare of our people here and abroad brought these points home to us. When we saw the well-meaning machinations of a host of lords whose overarching activities integrated vast regions of this globe under their control, we could understand why our efforts were outmaneuvered. When we compared the promises of friends to their actual performances, or compared intentions to outcomes, even the brightest and most dedicated were outwitted at critical points by principalities and powers. One was not being thankless toward sacrificial friends by saying this. One was only being honest, and hoping that sobriety and humility could prevail among more of the activists we appreciated at many points as we worked with them.

Because of these considerations many of us experimented with other portions of the Bible. We found ourselves appreciating the very books that our highly respected teachers found most problematic. Occasionally they would appeal to historic figures like Martin Luther who rejected the very books we found so helpful. For example, we appreciated the story of Esther. Although she had assimilated herself into an alien society by denying her ethnic identity, her cousin, Mordecai, challenged her to reassert it. Esther eventually reversed the decrees against her own people by risking her life in an illegal act.

We also recovered a use for Daniel and Revelation. Daniel

described the advancement of bicultural aliens in a foreign land. They were not, however, deluded into forgetting the creaturely status of the Golden Age of the Empire that hosted them. Nor did they neglect witnessing to the demise of the Empire because of its price and injustices. Such witnesses may be costly, but we saw in Daniel a call to faithfulness, not success.

Revelation, like Daniel, recalled what God did when intermediaries positioned themselves between the Creator and the creatures. The intermediaries are not God. When their pretensions hamper God from fulfilling the best that is possible, God rectifies whatever has gone awry. We read in the biblical witness of the compassionate God who seeks Shalom in place of cowering acquiescence under tyrannies, of the Merciful One who works relentlessly until domination and exploitation give way to justice, and of the God of truth who is astir until false promises and fraud which permeate human societies are overcome with what is trustworthy and true. We are called in Revelation to witness to this living God and invited to participate in that awesome but promising drama of creating a new heaven and a new earth when God will wipe away every tear, and death shall be no more, neither shall there be mourning nor pain, for the former things will pass away. God will thus dwell in the human family (Rev. 21:3–4).

While exploring the potential uses of these neglected portions of the Bible, I participated in a national denominational panel on ethics. I was asked for the biblical foundations to the suggestions I offered. Apparently other participants thought the suggestions were reckless. When I cited Esther, Daniel, and Revelation, they seemed even more startled and summarily dismissed the earlier offerings I made in the discussion. I was somewhat deflated because the panelists included several revered teachers and nationally recognized preachers. I took consolation, however, in the validation I received earlier from Koreans. I asked them for the biblical grounds that sustained the people in their decades of resistance against Japanese colonial policies and subsequent repressive regimes. One of their leaders answered without hesitation: "Exodus, Esther, Daniel, and Revelation!"

What startled me at the time was that we had been working in the Asian American community with the same biblical witnesses to

God's activities and calling. I welcomed this validation. I subsequently learned that the Japanese colonial government promulgated a polity that prohibited the use of these very books in worship services or prayer meetings. I continued to respect my esteemed teachers and recognized preachers at other points, but consciously chose to salvage for our people the very portions of the Bible that they rejected. Because these books acknowledged the intermediaries that can operate between God and the created order, they depicted the course of events in which God acts and clarified our calling. We found the map that took account of the terrain we were traversing and thus offered a better guide for action.

4. *Deliverance First, Then the Covenant.* One of the fundamental changes in reading the Bible can be illustrated in the use of the literature associated with the exile when the Children of Israel were captive to the Babylonians (587–538 B.C.E.). This includes such books as Jeremiah, Ezekiel, Isaiah (particularly chaps. 40–66), Haggai, and Zechariah (especially chaps. 1–8). Again, this body of writings is associated with the time when the Jewish people were coming under the domination of an alien power, making their way through their captivity, or recovering from it. In the words of this essay, they were dealing with intermediaries that had emerged between themselves and their God. Again, we can ask what does God do under these circumstances and what are we called to do?

As one follows the usual summaries of this body of literature, one frequently notices an attention to the covenant and its cognate concept. In other words, they are preoccupied with the way God reestablishes a covenant, or rebinds God's Self, with the people. These studies proceed as if the intermediaries did not exist or could not present any problem. The biblical writers on their part, however, are very clear that unless those "hosts of lords" were moved out of the way or subjected to God's reign, God could not be the Lord of the Hosts. That is, unless God is Lord of the Hosts over the hosts of the lords, Israel could not be people *of* God. They would still be subjected to the reign of lesser gods and lords who could not deliver the justice, mercy, truth, and peace that only God as Lord (Sovereign or Prevailer) provides.

One can turn to almost any commentary, whether technical or

popular, and find how pervasive this contrast is between biblical students and the Bible itself. We can take Jeremiah, for example. Most studies will focus on the New Covenant in Jer. 31:33–34.

> This is the covenant which I will make with the house of Israel after those days, says the Lord: I will put my law within them, and I will write it upon their hearts; and I will be their God and they shall be my people. And no longer shall each man teach his neighbor and teach his brother saying, 'Know the Lord,' for they shall all know me, from the least of them to the greatest, says the Lord; for I will forgive their iniquity and I will remember their sin no more (Jer. 31:33–34; see, too, Ezek. 36:25–28).

Our attention is frequently directed to this passage because it summarizes an understanding of the saving work of God that has dominated European and North American Christianity. We find (1) forgiveness of sins, (2) changing of people's character by writing God's law within, and (3) perfecting that work so that people will not need to teach each other to do God's will. In accomplishing these ends, they will become God's people, and the Lord (Yahweh) will become their God. In corresponding theological terms, salvation includes (1) justification, (2) sanctification, and (3) perfection or consummation. The end result is reconciliation, or a covenant (bonding or binding) between the people and God.

These are all very important experiences within God's saving activities. However, notice what happens if we take as a point of departure the characteristic of our situation which we are highlighting in this report of changes in reading the Bible among Asian Americans. If we take into account the domination of intermediaries that have emerged between ourselves and our God, God's salvation must include something more than the covenant or reconciliation. Unless we are delivered first from the domination of the hosts of lords, we cannot be people *of* God. Jeremiah recognized this and thus spoke of another exodus before there could be any meaningful talk about a new covenant. Preoccupation with reconciliation which characterizes U.S. Protestantism usually misses this crucial step in a fuller picture of the story of salvation in Jeremiah.

> "And it shall come to pass in that day," says the Lord of hosts, "that I will break the yoke from off their neck, and I will burst their bonds, and strangers shall no more make servants of them. But they shall

serve the Lord their God and David their king whom I will raise up for them" (Jer. 30:3-9, or Jer. 31:31-32 in the setting of the passage cited earlier; see too, Ezek. 34:27-28).

God is clearly promising a deliverance or liberation from the domination they experienced under the Babylonians. It recalls the exodus when they were emancipated from the bondage to the Egyptian yoke of slavery. This new deliverance, however, will make them forget that earlier experience, according to Jeremiah.

> "Therefore, behold, the days are coming," says the Lord, "when people shall no longer say, 'As the Lord lives who brought up the people of Israel out of the land of Egypt,' but 'As the Lord lives who brought up and led the descendants of the house of Israel and of the North country and out of all the countries where he had driven them.' Then they shall dwell in their own land" (Jer. 27:7-8, adapted; see, too, Ezek. 36:23-24).

Whether they remember the original exodus from Egypt or can only recall their most recent liberation from the Babylonians, these passages highlight the deliverance or redemption that makes it possible to speak of a meaningful reconciliation. That is, how could the people be genuinely reconciled or bound to their God when they are in bondage to hosts of lords? Only if the intermediaries are subjected to the reign of God, unless the people are delivered from the domination of alien powers, can we say they are reconciled to their God.

The point I have been making is that the situation that our social analysis brought to our attention made us alert to aspects of the story of salvation that our teachers frequently overlooked or failed to highlight. This fuller picture of the course of events in which we can find God acting uncovered for us a new calling. If we are to participate in God's saving actions, we are not only called to experience reconciliation, along with (1) forgiveness, (2) a new law within, and (3) the perfection of that process. We are called to participate with God in the redemptive events of deliverance, liberation, and emancipation from domination under intermediaries. This picture of the stories of salvation does not only describe what we were encountering in the hosts of lords and principalities and powers, it depicts what God would do under the circumstances and beckons us to do as well. These accounts presented a new picture of God and a new script for us. We have very clearly moved into the use of theological resources in our reflections.

FAITH IN A CHANGED CONTEXT

Recovering Traditional Theological Terms

I have directed attention to our theological understanding of salvation. Our rereading of the Bible has suggested that we add to the usual preoccupation with "reconciliation" another condition or step which I have called "redemption." We can now move from this focus on salvation to a focus on the Savior. If our picture of salvation has dwelt on reconciliation, it does not surprise us that the predominant understanding of Jesus as Savior has looked to him as Reconciler, or Mediator. The approach followed here suggests that Jesus is not only Reconciler, but Redeemer as well—not only Mediator, but Liberator as well. If we are followers of this Jesus, we are called to participate in redemption as well as reconciliation, liberation as well as mediation. Because of this line of reflection on the biblical and theological resources, "liberation theologies" did not come as a fad to many of us who were involved in the human rights struggles during the 1970s or the movements for racial justice in the 1960s. We saw how integral redemption, deliverance, emancipation, and liberation were to the witness of our forebears. And we were therefore aware of their appropriateness to feminists who helped us see the domination of sexism that pervaded our societies and our psyches. In each of these cases—whether on the issues of sexism, racism, or neocolonialism, God was acting as redeemer and reconciler. God beckoned us to join in the same struggles.

Making the Profane Sacred

It is worth mentioning one additional way we rehabilitated the ancient tradition of the church. In this case we were not adding a distinct category of title to God, but recovering ingredients in an existing title which we had missed. We felt as if we had committed something of a profanity in our earlier assertions. When we discovered the biblical picture of Jesus as the God Mighty to Save, we felt as if our earlier limitation on salvation from personal sins turned Jesus into a trivial Savior. We recognized in the witness of our biblical forebears the Lord of hosts who was bent on prevailing over and permeating the hosts of lords (Heb. 2:5–8, 10:13) with justice and truth, love and mercy. Our earlier affirmations sounded as if we were speaking of a lord of a small manor.

We pursued many other lines of reflections. These illustrations, however, should suffice to indicate the changes in our faith that occurred. As is evident by now, changes took place in the picture of the world in which we were living—our context changed. The biblical and theological resources helped us see more fully what God was doing in the course of events we uncovered and helped us recognize God's call in them.

Prompting Mutuality in Mission

I have already cited a number of things I did with the new discoveries in our context. Two summary consequences are worth elaboration. I found in this approach a new basis for *mutuality in mission* as well as possibilities for renewed spirituality. Mutuality in mission is very important to those of us who have been "objects of mission." We know the subtle but degrading consequences of condescension in much of our mission and ministry. The endemic disease appears as paternalism, as well as maternalism, and knows no boundaries of class, race, or theological stripe. It appears in the church as well as in the community.

References to "power line" speak to this issue. Power arrangements are such today that I do not believe anyone of us can say that we are fully *above* the power line. There are, however, differences that we can draw between those who are manipulated blatantly and those who are managed subtly but forcefully when it comes to matters that truly count. Corporations will allow us to dabble in social responsibility—up to a point. In that sense, we are under the power line. I have also referred to the differences between those *above* and those *below* the "poverty line." Just because we are below the power line, I am not suggesting that there are no significant differences within the human family concerning the basic necessities of life. The poverty line is a most telling difference we cannot dismiss among those of us living under the power line.

What I am suggesting, however, is that if we recognize the seriousness of the power line overhead for all of us, then we have substantive grounds for solidarity or mutuality in mission. We all "begin from below" when it comes to the important elements in the distribution of power. Even liberation theologians can betray a subtle condescension when they speak of "solidarity with the poor" if they only see themselves "reaching down and pulling up" those who are "down and out." If they recognize the power line overhead, and also begin "reaching up and pulling down" the pretenders to God's reign, their poverty-stricken "objects of mission" might experience greater solidarity or mutuality in mission with them.

Furthermore, those of us who choose to remain in the established position of limited or apparent power cannot think of ourselves as technocrats—although many do. We are not in a position where we can say we will push a button here or pull a handle there and the desired changes will take place. We should all be well beyond that stage of "thinking of ourselves more highly than we ought." Sad to say, however, the most socially and ethically sensitive—the most progressive in visions of future possibilities—are sometimes the most presumptuously technocratic. We still think we are in charge and all that is required is our enlightened action. The line of reflection followed here suggests that we are not in charge. Unless we participate, from below, with the God Mighty to Save in that grand drama of rectifying what has gone wrong, we are at best shadowboxers.

One of the ironies of human experience is that those who come to this consciousness of their powerlessness or a recognition of the limits to their power become the most transparent media for new visions. They begin influencing the course of events because they unleash dimensions of the divine activity and energize human efforts in ways that were unexpected. That is why they are likely to say, "It is God who has made us and not we ourselves" (see Ps. 100:3). That line is not a pious platitude, but one of the most hallowing and humanizing utterances we can make.

Thus, the *spiral of action and reflection* cannot only foster *mutuality in mission* because all of us begin from below. It also cultivates a sanctity or spirituality that hallows this desecrated island home in the universe. So let it be, dear God, so let it be. Amen.

5
WHAT IS CONTEXTUAL THEOLOGY?

ROBERT McAFEE BROWN

My own introduction to contextual theology—or more properly to the realization that I was not doing it even when I didn't yet know the term—came at the first Theology of the Americas Conference in Detroit in the summer of 1975. About midway through the conference, which for the first time brought together significant numbers of North and South American theologians, I was in a small group of North Americans conversing with Gonzalo Arroyo, a Chilean Jesuit who had had to flee for his life after the military coup by General Pinochet. Fr. Arroyo said to us, more out of curiosity than pique, "Why is it that when you talk about *our* position you call it 'Latin American theology,' but when you talk about *your* position you call it 'theology'?" And although his question took us aback, we had (at least privately) to acknowledge its appropriateness. For we were assuming, implicitly at least, that our position was the norm, the true distillation of the gospel, and that his position was an interesting, even exotic, cultural variant indulged in by people "down there" whose perspective was obviously influenced by their geographical, historical, and cultural situation, whereas ours, of course, was free of such contextual coloration and distortion. He was contextual, we were normative; score one for us.

If we are even going to begin to think contextually, and let that sort of thinking help mold our theology, the presupposition we must accept is that our own position, whatever it is, is *not* normative, but is itself the product of many factors that may heretofore have escaped our notice: our race, class, sex, economic status, geographical location, or whatever. It is this awareness of our own context that, as I shall argue later, can liberate us from seeking to exercise over others a kind of theological imperialism that is at best unthinking and shallow and at worst ugly and destructive.

(I say this in full knowledge that I, a white male North American middle-class academician, symbolize that group in the theological world who have sinned most in failing to acknowledge the contextual nature of our own theologizing, and have initially been resistant to acknowledging the full legitimacy of the newly articulated contexts from within which others are now theologizing—blacks, Asians, Hispanics, feminists, gays, lesbians, Third World poor, and so on. That such a one is invited to contribute to this book is a mark of the forbearance of those who have been most sinned against.)

SETTING THE PROBLEM

Let us begin by juxtaposing two familiar passages from Scripture that set our problem. The first is a statement of the content and power of the gospel: "Jesus Christ [is] the same, yesterday, today, and forever" (Heb. 11:8b). The second is a statement about those who receive and transmit the gospel: "For we have this treasure in earthen vessels" (2 Cor. 4:7).

And there we have the two sides of the contextual coin. The gospel viewpoint is eternal, but enfleshed. We are enfleshed, but our viewpoint is not eternal; it is mediated through "earthen vessels." As a result, there will always be a distance between what we proclaim as the gospel, and what the gospel itself actually is. At our best, we will achieve approximations, pointers, "hints and guesses," as T. S. Eliot puts it. The treasure we have is in "earthen vessels"— "clay pots" is a more literal and humbling translation.

This is not necessarily a bad thing. In fact, in terms of the meaning of the gospel it is a supremely good thing, as St. Paul goes on to say in the Second Corinthian letter: "We have this treasure in earthen vessels. . . . " Why? "To show that the transcendent power belongs to God and not to us" (2 Cor. 4:7). If it were not for the "clay pots" disclaimer, we would be tempted to believe that the transcendent power belonged to us, or at least that we were in control of it. We would be tempted, in other words, to confuse the message, that is, Jesus Christ, with the messenger, that is, ourselves. But as St. Paul lays it out, we are forced to acknowledge that if "Jesus Christ is the same yesterday, today, and forever," our understandings of him are not, but need constant revision, deepening, and broadening, as we grow in faith, as we see how cultural overlays, our narrow contexts, have distorted who he is.

THE BUILT-IN CONTEXTUALITY OF CHRISTIAN FAITH

Let us examine this consideration from within the faith claim itself. The very nature of the claim Christians make is inconceivable save contextually. For the Jesus Christ who is "the same yesterday, today, and forever" is not an eternal principle, a timeless truth, to be sought in some realm removed from time, contingency, mud, carnality, and power struggles. On the contrary, the conditions under which information about him became available to us represent contextuality run riot. The one who is "the same yesterday, today, and forever" becomes known to us through a first-century Jew, one who lived for only a few years, never traveled more than fifty miles from the place of his birth, and left no written records. (The only thing he is reported to have written was written in sand, hardly a substance designed to preserve messages for eternity.) Most of what he said was in immediate and ad hoc situations, when lawyers, religious leaders, and other assorted sinners were trying to put him on the spot and trap him. The only records we have about him share this same casual quality—a few brief accounts, a handful of letters hastily dictated by a convert, none of them even written in the classical language of the time, but simply in a back-country dialect.

And it is the very nature of the faith-claim that makes such facts both appropriate and inevitable. Faiths that proclaim epiphanies, that is, stories of gods temporarily appearing before mortal gaze and then withdrawing, cannot afford to be contextual; they must record a vision of the eternal untrammeled by the trappings of mortality, or else they play their vision false. But a faith that proclaims incarnation, that is, the story of a God fully and completely indwelling a human life, so human that the one enfleshed gets tired, hungry, discouraged, weeps, loses faith (at least temporarily), and dies an ignominious death—such a faith by its very nature *must* be contextual, all wrapped up in the tendencies of the time and place within which it is set. To describe it, we have to refer to contemporary political figures like "Pontius Pilate" in the midst of our most solemn creedal affirmations, and we have to use immediate and earthy verbs like "born," "suffered," "crucified," "dead," and "buried." There is nothing ethereal in such a message. Everything is here-and-now, nitty-gritty, embedded in a particular time, place, culture, and context. To say, "The Word became flesh and dwelt among us" is to proclaim a gospel that is contextual by its very nature.

THREE MEANINGS OF CONTEXT

Recognizing, then, that the gospel itself is incurably and designedly contextual from the start, let us now seek to give more precision to our central term. There are two basic dictionary definitions of the word "context" at which we must look briefly in order to flesh out what they mean for theology, and then we must create a third definition, lacking in our dictionaries, that is probably the most important of all theologically.

The Latin verb *texo, texui, textum* means "to weave." When we place *con-* in front of it, meaning "with" (from the Latin *cum*), we come up with the notion of weaving together, intertwining, plaiting, and so forth. The late medieval noun *contextus* suggests "a joining together." So to speak about a "context" is to speak about juxtaposing otherwise separate things, putting them together in ways that show their relationship.

1. From these reflections we derive an initial meaning of "context" as we use it in English. It refers to *"the parts of a written or spoken statement* that precede or follow a specific word or passage, usually influencing its meaning or effect."[1]

If that seems a bit abstract, remember our immediate gut-level, pained reaction when somebody quotes us and misrepresents us. "But you've taken what I said *out of context!*" we respond defensively. "If you'd read the whole passage, you'd see what I mean, and it's not at all what you say it is."

A famous example in our time of out-of-context quoting is the bromide of armchair anti-Marxists, Marx's statement that "religion is the opium of the people." "Ahah," the critics say, "we've nailed Marx to the wall. To him religion is like shooting cocaine." But the statement *in its context* conveys a very different message: "Religious distress," Marx wrote, "is at the same time the expression of real distress and the protest against real distress. Religion is the sign of the oppressed creature, the heart of a heartless world, just as it is the spirit of a spiritless situation. It is the opium of the people."[2]

As Herbert Aptheker comments on misuse of this passage, it is exactly as though after the hostile crowd had melted away, we were to quote Jesus as saying to the woman taken in adultery, "Neither do I condemn thee, go and sin" (John 8:11a), when the full exhortation, in context, goes, "Neither do I condemn thee, go and sin no more" (John 8:11ab). The example illustrates the importance of our initial understanding of context; the obligation to remember, in the words of the definition, that "the parts of a written or spoken statement that precede or follow a specific word or passage" do inevitably influence its "meaning or effect."

I think we have learned this particular lesson pretty well. We know the importance of *seeing a text in context,* that is, in relation to the words that surround it, and we have learned that the more we know about the location of a passage in one of the gospels—Is it part of the passion narrative? Is it imbedded in the resurrection account, and if so, which one? Does it come from the teaching material assigned to "Q"? What is its *Sitz im leben* in the narrative?—the more likely we are to approximate its original meaning and avoid distortion.

2. But there is a second definition of context that is important theologically, which goes, *"the set of circumstances or facts* that surround a particular event, situation, etc." This widens the area of interweaving; we not only have to take account of the inner construction of the text (whether a canonical writing, a creedal affirmation, or simply a theological essay), but also the outer circumstances under which the text came into being. We must explore this meaning in more detail.

With some assurance, for example, we can date the first thirty-nine chapters of Isaiah as coming from a different and earlier historical period than those that follow. This enables us to hear, with even greater poignancy and power, Isaiah 40 with its promises of strength and restitution, for we know that the latter words are addressed to people in exile, and we know something about the stringent conditions of their exile. Such information enhances the power of the verses for us.

When we study the Nicene Creed, to take another example, it is not enough simply to determine the inner logic of the document, how the various affirmations flow into and from one another, what kind of verbs predominate, what rhythm and direction the text itself possesses—all of which is subsumed under the initial meaning of "context" that we have examined. It is also necessary to know as much as possible about the time and place in which the document was conceived—the "circumstances," as the dictionary definition puts it—if the full meaning of the creed is to emerge for us. The creed offers certain affirmations, certain assurances, certain "answers." To understand, let alone appropriate them fully, we need to know what questions were being asked in that period of the church's life to which the Nicene answers seemed necessary. Since creeds usually arise in the life of the church to protect aspects of the faith threatened by contemporary heresies, the more we know about the threatening heresies of the moment, the more we will be able to understand why a particular creedal affirmation was phrased in the particular way it has come down to us. We need also to understand what aspects of the faith were unchallenged at the time and could therefore be presupposed rather than spelled out once again in the new formulation.

It follows that if our situation and our questions are different from the situation and questions of the creedal formulators, we are likely to hear their affirmations in a different sense than they themselves intended. People today who look at the christological claims of the Christian faith, for example, are likely to approach them with the twentieth-century question, How could a human being be divine? To us, Jesus' humanity is no problem; Jesus' divinity is. But in the climate of the fourth-century creedal controversies, with challenges from movements like docetism and gnosticism, the prevailing question to be answered was a very different one, namely, How could a divine being possibly have been human? To them, Jesus' divinity was no problem; Jesus' humanity was. Only by taking full account of the historical circumstances of the development of the creed can we do full justice to its affirmations.

This recognition of the contextuality of historical theological affirmations (which applies to the biblical materials as well) points to an inherent limitation in our employment of them. For they, too, are examples of the earthen vessels in which the gift of "Jesus Christ, the same yesterday, today, and forever" is transmitted to us. At our theological and existential peril do we equate even such impressive vessels with the One whom they cannot fully contain? This means, bluntly, that there is no way we can ever claim that a statement about God, no matter how impressive its ecclesiological pedigree, is an adequate statement. Helpful though it may be, it will be less than adequate on at least two counts: (a) that it is a product of its own time, and thereby limited by the finite, not to say sinful, understanding of the time and persons who produced it, and (b) that it can never in the nature of the case do full justice to its subject matter, who is the God to whom alone, as St. Paul reminds us, the transcendent power belongs.

How, then, are we to make creative use of theological affirmation (whether canonical, creedal, confessional, or merely professional), given these limitations? I propose that we make a virtue out of the necessity imposed upon us, and aggressively expose ourselves to *varieties* of statements about "Jesus Christ, the same yesterday, today, and forever." Recognizing that they are all time-bound, less than exhaustive, and reflecting their own circumstantial creation, we can use them all as offering a variety of approaches to a subject matter that is admittedly inexhaustible.

Whether by chance or providence, for example, it was a stroke of genius on the part of the creators of the biblical canon to give us four separate accounts of Jesus' life, ministry, death, and resurrection, rather than just one, for the different accounts provide cross-checks for us, giving us a fuller picture of the claims about Jesus and the church than we would have if we had been limited to any one, two, or even three of them. Would we like more than four? Of course, for as the latest of the accounts concludes, "There are also many other things which Jesus did; were every one of them to be written, I suppose that the world itself could not contain the books that would be written" (John 21:25). The same thing is true of the multiplicity of our creeds and confessions, for it is obvious that the church has never been able to arrive at the point of saying, Now we have a fully adequate creed. The church must always keep on trying to say what it will never be able to say adequately. It may seem a problem to us that there are so many creeds and confessions, but a far greater problem would emerge if the church stopped writing them.

Let me give an example of a creative appropriation of these divergent witnesses. My own denomination (which at the time of the event I wish to cite was called the United Presbyterian Church in the United States of America) was for generations handcuffed to a single confessional statement, the Westminster Confession of 1648, which, whatever good can be said of it, was the most wooden and scholastic of the Reformation confessions. Ordinands had to affirm their belief that this confession, and this confession alone, contained *"the* system of doctrine taught in Holy Scripture." Over three centuries, only tiny adaptations were introduced to take account of changing perceptions. Not until 1903, for example, did the church add a footnote to the original text stating that the Pope was no longer to be considered the antichrist, and affirm that unbaptized babies dying in infancy were not consigned to hell—a generous concession that one hopes was made retroactive to include babies dying before 1903.

When our denomination's relationship to this Confession reached a potential breaking point, a committee was formed to write a new confessional statement more in keeping with perceptions of the faith today. But instead of offering a single new confession to which strict adherence would be demanded (with the implication that the earthen vessel was still equivalent to the transcendent power of God), the committee assembled a variety of confessions, and proposed that since our faith as Christians can never be exhaustively contained within a single document, we would be better advised to draw our inspiration from what we considered the best attempts over the centuries to articulate the faith in "Jesus Christ, the same yesterday, today, and forever." As a result, eight such statements were gathered—two from the undivided church (the Apostles' and Nicene Creeds), four from the Reformation (the Westminster Confession, the Shorter Catechism, the Second Helvetic Confession, and the Scots Confession), and two from our own era (the Barmen Declaration of the German Confessing Church in 1934, and the committee's own document, presented with the rather uninspiring title of the "Confession of 1967").

Such a procedure continues to affirm belief in "Jesus Christ, the same yesterday, today, and forever," since all the creeds and confessions noted above point unerringly to him, but it also acknowledges that we need multiple ways of asserting that claim, since every attempt to describe and point to him is limited by the context out of which it was first produced.

The process will have to continue. In 1967, the note of the gospel that particularly needed to be struck seemed to the authors of the Confession of 1967 to be *reconciliation,* and the confession is built around it as a central theme. Perhaps in our day, Christians in other parts of the world will try to restate the faith around the central theme of the good news of *liberation.* I hope at least that they will try, so that the rest of us can have the partiality of our own viewpoints further challenged and thereby expanded.

So far we have dealt with two understandings of "context": the context of written statements in relation to what precedes or follows them in the documents themselves, and context as the circumstances surrounding a particular event or situation that influence and shape the document.

3. There is a third definition of context, however, that is even more cynical in our own time, and it is one that the dictionary does not mention. I will call it the context of *the contemporary participant,* and in the style of the dictionary definitions thus far offered, defines it as follows: "the set of circumstances from which *we* view either a statement itself or the circumstances out of which it comes, and the set of circumstances out of which we speak for ourselves."

This is what Gonzalo Arroyo was trying to point out when he implied that if we North Americans were going to describe his position as "Latin American theology," that was fair enough so long as we also described our own position as "North American theology." If we perceived his theology as influenced by his context, seen by us to be a situation of oppression, Marxist analysis, and Hispanic culture, he wanted us to be aware that our theology was similarly influenced by our context, seen by him as a nation of oppressors, dominated by laissez faire economic analysis and a capitalist, materialist culture.

And yet even such awareness does not do full justice to the complexity of the situation. For if there is no such thing as *a* "Latin American theology," there is similarly no such thing as *a* "North American theology." There are only a bewildering variety of North American theolog*ies*. Certainly the dominance of white male middle-class theology is being challenged, even in North America—"that powerful bastion of male privilege"—although not all the white male middle-class dominators have yet gotten the message. Some of the best corrections of that myopic vision have come from North American blacks, women, Asians, Hispanics, gays, and lesbians, for example, all of whom have been rightly insisting that their situation, that is, their "context," is at least as legitimate a context in which to do theology as that of white males (and perhaps, in view of the nature of the biblical message, an even more legitimate context), but also that those theologizing from all of those contexts are delinquent in their duty if they fail to take account of this variety of perspectives and approaches.

WAYS OF DEALING CREATIVELY
WITH CONTEXTUALITY

How can we begin to deal with this bewildering, often confusing, situation? Let us examine half a dozen considerations that might help us use our present context creatively in the next stage of our collective theological enterprise.

1. *Our own context, as we behold and interpret what others have done, strongly influences our interpretation of what others have done.* This poses the familiar historical-textual problem of exegesis vs. eisegesis, that is, what can legitimately be drawn out of a text, and what we illegitimately read into it. In attempting to determine what a text says (whether canonical, creedal, or confessional), we are always in danger of imposing on the text what we want to hear and expunging from it whatever we don't want to hear.

Examples abound. In affluent cultures, exegetes persuade us that when Jesus talked about "good news to the poor," he meant not the materially poor but the spiritually poor, which, of course, includes all of us. By conflating the two concepts into one, a skillful exegete can persuade us that we don't have to do anything about the materially poor, since spiritual riches are what really count, and we can all have spiritual riches whether we are affluent or poverty-stricken. The evangelistic task, from this perspective, is to persuade everyone to be content with his or her lot, and look forward to the spiritual kingdom that comes to the truly devout whatever their outward earthly circumstances. *In oppressed cultures,* on the other hand, exegetes (who are usually the poor themselves rather than professional theologians or Scripture scholars) hear the words about "good news to the poor" as liberating on *all* levels—political and economic as well as interior—and remind their listeners how centrally the gospel focuses on this theme, since careful exegetical study suggests that in both testaments the "poor" to whom good news is addressed are those conspicuously lacking in material resources.

A test case in relation to these two approaches: what is our instinctive recollection of the "Magnificat"? Is it a beautiful poem (to which we probably know several musical settings) by a humble maiden who is obedient to the voice of an angel and thus becomes a willing and almost passive instrument of the Holy Spirit? Or is it a revolutionary manifesto by one who announces, with fire in her eye, that God has put down the mighty from their thrones, exalted those of low degree, filled the hungry with good things, and sent the rich empty away?

2. *Our context as beholder involves the risk of making us beholden.* Mark Twain recalls a boyhood friend who used to preach to him from the top of the woodpile, and whose text went, "You tell me what a man gets his corn pone from, an' I'll tell you what his 'pinion is." (I have not yet tracked this text down in our canonical Scriptures, even with the help of a large concordance. If it is not in the Bible, it ought to be.)

We see this tendency clearly when examining the context of others, and are frequently tempted to ad hominem remarks about how in their case the one who pays the piper calls the tune. I have come to feel, for example, that a former colleague and friend of mine is now beholden to, and the captive of, big business. But if

I make such an assessment, it may turn out to be the case that the shoe fits on my foot as well, and that I am beholden to something else. If I am, I can be sure that my friend will so inform me. As we engage in our theologizing, in other words, we need to face as honestly as we can the question: to whom are we really beholden? Is it solely to the transcendent God revealed in Jesus Christ, or do we have supplementary agendas of our own that warp such beholdenness? Whose interests are we defending by the way we do theology? Who is providing the corn pone? Who is most likely to benefit by our theological conclusions? ourselves? folks like us? the Church? the corporations? the revolution? When we confuse the earthen vessels with the God they cannot contain, we have become imprisoned by our contexts.

3. *We tend to absolutize our contexts* with the result that we seek to make them normative for others. An amusing, and fortunately dated, example of this occurred in Rome during Vatican II. A request had come from some of the missionary bishops that as long as procedures for saying mass were under review, they be permitted, back in their missionary situations, to offer mass in midafternoon. The request was turned down by a Rome-based Curia official as unrealistic. This reason: no one would be served by such a change, since midafternoon is the time everyone takes a siesta.

Even with the best will in the world, we allow our contexts to continue to form who we are. A visitor came to lecture in my class recently, and engaged in an open and instructive discussion with the students about sexist language—a problem he acknowledged hadn't even been on the theological or human horizon when he went to seminary. He gave many signals of hearing the women's concerns, affirmed that he was doing his best to understand and be responsive to them, and then blew it all by concluding, "I pray about this every morning. 'Father,' I pray, 'help me. . . . ' "

In more serious ways than these, we continue to make our own contexts normative for others. Men continue to try to speak for women; white North Americans claim authority to represent the concerns of Third World peoples; gays and lesbians find themselves treated condescendingly by those who say in effect, "Look, I love you even though. . . . "

Within the recent life of the world church, a theme has been predominent in World Council reports and papal pronouncements, asserting that "it is the task of the church to be 'the voice of the voiceless.'" This may once have been a noble theme, but it is now becoming clear that there is something highly condescending in the notion that *we* are the only ones who are truly able to speak for *them*. Surely the church will have come to the beginnings of maturity on such matters only when it can say: our task is to provide the voiceless with a place in which and from which they can speak on their own behalf.

4. In order to overcome the blind spots, the flawed perspectives, the failures of understanding, *we need firsthand exposure to other contexts than our own,* so that we can not only understand them but also have our own understanding transformed by them. The sheer human responsibility of understanding another's position is a prerequisite here, but the other part of the task is even more important, namely, allowing our own perspectives to be opened up, challenged, and transformed by immediate contact with the perspective of the other. This is not a comfortable position to espouse, and I say it as a white male, one of those who has the most to lose, initially at least, by such an acknowledgment. For a long, long time, theology was a white male preserve. We were dominant. And we thought that "dominant" equaled "normative." Now that that has been challenged, we are obliged, with whatever grace we can muster, not only to acknowledge past sins, but to step to the side or at least share the stage.

We would never have reached this conclusion on our own. I fear there is not that much grace still resident in wounded male egos. It takes challenge, sometimes strident, sometimes healing, of other contexts to reveal to us the partiality, the limitedness, and therefore the blindness, of our own. But if we have had the most to lose initially, we also have the most to gain ultimately, because we can begin to see beyond what were very limited perspectives. Those closest to blindness have greatest cause for rejoicing at the restoration of sight.

5. *We must be careful not to confuse contextualization with relativization.* Those who most fear contextual theology usually assume that contextualization and relativization are the same

thing, and that the enduring gospel is being whittled away by relativistic assertions that boil down to saying, "I say it my way, you say it your way, somebody else says it a third way. Take your pick, it's all relative."

This misses the point, and is a consequence of the very confusion that contextual theology is trying to overcome, that is, confusing the gospel with the vessels in which it is transmitted. The point is not that there are many gospels, but that there is *one gospel that can be stated in many ways.* And since there are many ways of appropriating it in human speech, we need exposure to a variety of ways, particularly so that the inadequacies of our way of stating it may be challenged and overcome, and we can all move closer to the real thing. We are not impoverished but enriched by the mutual sharing of our different contexts.

To return to an earlier example, I cannot help but understand the "Magnificat" better if I am forced to hear it through Third World ears as well as my own. I cannot help but know God better if I am confronted by the need to acknowledge not only paternal but also maternal images of God that I've never been aware of before. That there is a male sexist bias on the part of some of the biblical writers is something I have needed help from feminists to discover. But all of us, whatever our dissimilar contexts, share the same Scriptures, and that is a potentially unifying point. For we can move along together to deal with the ultimate meaning of an image like *Abba,* which happens to mean "daddy," but which may be recoverable as an image pointing to an intimacy of personal relationship between God and ourselves that is richer for us by being stripped of exclusively male associations in our mind. If so, there will be enrichment rather than diminution.

6. *What does all this mean about our own contexts?* I think that for now it means being as up front as we can about our own contexts, acknowledging them, seeking to see how they both inform and limit our perspectives, so that in that spirit we can be open to the contribution of other contexts to our own understanding. We make our greatest initial contribution by insisting that our own contexts be taken into account and not too prematurely molded into a new kind of theological homogeneity. We can be sure that establishment theology has not yet heard enough from blacks,

gays, lesbians, women, Asians, Hispanics, and all the rest. There are surely some strident times still ahead, because as establishment positions are increasingly challenged, and the full implications of moving aside from power positions become clearer, the tendency of establishment defenders to institutional and personal stonewalling will increase.

But a time will come, we can hope, when the acknowledgment of the limited insights of our own positions, and the new insights of other positions, can be appropriated with more joy than apprehension. That may take a long time, and maybe only in heaven will we have enough security to surrender our individual earthen vessels to the demolition squad. But wider perspectives are always possible, and even those fulfilled only in heaven can sometimes, when glimpsed, be transferred to earth.

A Hasidic tale makes this point more perceptively than further abstractions: It is a time of great rejoicing in heaven. The Israelites have just escaped through the Red Sea and Pharaoh's army has drowned. So the angels are singing and dancing. How often, after all, have there been Jewish victories to celebrate? But God is not singing or dancing. God is weeping. Noticing this, the archangel Michael approaches the divine throne and addresses the Almighty: "There has been a great victory," he says. "Why are you weeping?"

And the voice from the divine throne responds, "Why should I not be weeping when so many of *my children* have drowned?"

NOTES

1. *Random House Dictionary,* unabridged ed. (New York: Random House, 1981), emphasis added.
2. Cited in Herbert Aptheker, *The Urgency of Christian-Marxist Dialogue* (New York: Harper & Row, 1970), 5.

SUGGESTIONS FOR STUDY
AND ACTION

Like ripples from a pebble dropped into a still pond, changes in our relationship of faith with God have an ever-widening circle of effect. Our neighbors at hand and around the globe are affected by the changes in our perceptions and actions as our relationship with a God who cares for the earth and for all God's creatures leads us to find new ways of working for social and personal wholeness. For this reason, *Changing Contexts of Our Faith* is a study book designed to be shared with others. As we are learning about our faith from the stories in the book, we can be telling our own stories of faith to others in our study or action groups. On the basis of our shared experiences we can reflect together on the biblical story of God's love in Jesus Christ, and search out the most creative actions that we might take together with others to share in God's concern for the mending of creation so that there will be peace with justice and human dignity among all people.

These suggestions for study and action are only a beginning step for the group study and action process. They point out ways that the book might be used as a resource for discussion. To facilitate reflection on the material in the chapters there are questions and suggestions for acting our way into new thinking. Finally there is a model for Bible study in context that can be used in conjunction with the material in this book or independently for group study.

Books suggested for reading and study are listed under "Additional Resources."

WAYS TO USE THIS BOOK

1. Group Study of the Book. Either a newly organized or an existing group can go through the chapters and questions using one for each session. In order to improve the discussion ask people to read the material ahead and come to the sessions with their own questions or with one chosen from this study guide. If possible, rotate the leadership of the sessions. Be sure to begin each session with reactions and questions and *not* with a lecture.

2. Resource Persons. Invite people who would be particularly interested in the story of each of the chapters to attend a session on that topic either as a resource person for discussion of the story, or as a presenter who could tell his or her own story of shifting perspective so that the group can "write its own chapter." For instance, someone who attended the Vancouver meeting of the WCC could share that story during the session on chapter 2; a woman might share her changing perceptions of the role of women in the church for chapter 3; an Asian American or a Korean might be invited for chapter 4; and someone who has shared in a Latin American, black, or feminist experience of theological reflection in context might attend the session in relation to chapter 5.

3. Story Telling. Rather than studying the book as such it would be possible to invite different persons in the group to share their faith stories and then to ask the same questions that were asked in the three "case studies" presented by Zikmund, Farmer, and Sano:
What was the person's view before it changed?
How was it influenced by her or his context?
What caused the change in perception?
What new awareness of faith and new actions resulted?

4. Social Analysis. Study the social issues that are raised in the "case studies" using resource materials from your denomination, from Friendship Press, or from magazines or media about the situations of injustice and exclusion that are experienced by Third World Christians, feminist Christians, Asian American Christians, or another group that suffers discrimination.

5. *Social Action*. Involve your group in peacemaking, working with refugees, upholding civil rights, working for a community rape crisis center, or any one of the countless areas of human need that call out for our actions. Use the meetings of the group to reflect on what is being learned through taking these actions and how this relates to the biblical message of justice and shalom.

6. *Bible Study*. Using the contextual model of study included in this study guide select biblical materials referred to in the chapters and create sessions of the group around study of the biblical texts.

GUIDE FOR ACTION REFLECTION

Introduction and Chapter 1:
Exploring the Contexts of Our Faith

The purpose of the introduction and chapter 1 is to explore the meaning of faith and how our faith is affected by changes in our surrounding communities and culture. They ask us what difference it makes in our commitment to God and neighbor when we see our faith in a new setting or context.

1. Sit quietly and recall moments of new insight or changes in perception that came to you from a change in your life experience. Those who are comfortable with sharing might tell their story to the group so it can be discussed.

2. Look up the word "faith" in a biblical concordance and each pick out the passage that means the most for her or him. These passages can then be shared and discussed.

3. James 2:26, Heb. 11:1 and 1 Cor. 13:13 each stress different aspects of faith as a relationship of knowing, acting, and trusting. Read these texts in their contexts and discuss how the context of the early church readers affected what the writers said about the meaning of faith.

4. Describe the social and religious context in which you grew up.

5. Visualize your life journey and think of three important turning points in that road and draw a picture of each one. Discuss how these turning points changed your understanding of God.

6. Listen together to one of the famous TV or radio preachers and discuss the context or setting of people's lives in which this message makes particularly good sense, and whether and how it makes sense to the group.

7. Describe the social, church, and theological context of your study group and discuss what effect this has on the way you live out the gospel.

Chapter 2: Expanding Horizons

The purpose of chapter 2 is to share one experience of a North American moving into an ecumenical and global setting. This new situation challenged her way of thinking about herself, her nation, and the world. This challenges us to look at the horizon of our own faith and to ask how that horizon might be expanded.

1. Visit a church service in a congregation that has a different racial, denominational, economic, or cultural background from your own. Discuss the differences you discover in the way they understand and articulate their faith in Jesus Christ.

2. Why is it that the gospel of Jesus Christ has to be interpreted anew in each new context?

3. Use one of the reports on the Assembly provided in the chapter notes or the set of slides on the Assembly that may be available for rent at your local audio-visual resource center. Discuss the work of the WCC and why it is that so many U.S. Christians consider their stand on justice issues to be a radical one.

4. Discuss experiences of going to another country or to an area where you do not understand the language spoken. How did this change in context challenge the preconceptions of the traveler?

5. Why do Americans frequently find that the United States is unpopular with people in Third World countries?

6. Ask someone from a Third World country to share their experience of the missionary movement in their country, and the unique problems of interpretation that arise for Christians in that culture.

7. Discuss possibilities that exist for expanding horizons in your

own city, town, or community, and plan to make use of these resources in order to challenge the church community to new actions and insights.

Chapter 3: Retelling the Story

The purpose of chapter 3 is to invite the readers to join in the discovery of what it means to be "included out." It raises the question of the authority of the Bible and tradition, asking how to be faithful in reinterpretation of the Christian message in changing circumstances.

1. Discuss the story and share your own stories of having someone ask you a question and realizing that you can no longer give the same old answer. What was the change in your own situation that caused "cognitive dissonance" between your experience and the way you name and understand things?

2. Try to pick out clues to the context of the author of the story. What things in her context do you think have influenced her point of view?

3. How would you have dealt with the child's question if you had been asked? Test out the question by asking small children in your church whether they think *men* means both men and women and *brothers,* both brother and sister when we sing such hymns as "Join hands then brothers of the faith. . . . "

4. How do women and girls participate in the life of your church? Who decides what they can or cannot do in your church? What is the basis of these decisions?

5. Give out hymnals to the group and have them all pick their favorite hymn. As people discuss why they like the hymns, notice how their own religious background affects their preferences. Look at the hymns to see which ones use language that is inclusive of women and men. Share examples of inclusive hymns from books such as *Ever Flowing Streams* and *Joy in Singing.*

6. Ask those in the group who have changed their minds about the importance of inclusive language to tell their "conversion" stories. Look at the *Inclusive Language Lectionary* Appendix and discuss the word substitutions made in the RSV Bible and why they decided to do this.

7. Discuss your own perspectives on some of the Bible passages quoted by Farmer about the role of women in the Bible. Books in "Additional Resources" such as those by Phyllis Trible, Rachel Conrad Whalberg, and Elisabeth Schüssler Fiorenza would be helpful here.

Chapter 4: Transforming Suffering

The purpose of this chapter is to share the experience of an Asian American of transforming suffering. Through the human rights struggles of Christians in South Korea, Sano discovered new faith perspectives and new commitment to action. This raises the question for us of our own willingness to confront structures of injustice, and how this relates to our calling as Christians.

1. Explore experiences that you might have had or read about that are similar to those reported in this story. Have you had the feeling yourself of seeing "principalities and powers" managing, if not manipulating, your life? Share moments that you were newly aware of these powerful forces such as during the Vietnam War, or the discovery of toxic wastes in a nearby neighborhood.

2. Review the references to Jeremiah and Ezekiel in the chapter and summarize in your own words what God does in the "new covenant." Give historic or contemporary examples of God's redemptive actions that might be comparable to the ones described in those texts. In what concrete ways might we participate in movements for redemption?

3. Invite a person who is a political refugee in this country to speak about their experience and investigate what churches are doing to help refugees and to provide sanctuary for them when they are in danger of deportation.

4. To experience more deeply the history and context of the suffering in South Korea, study the book *Fire Beneath the Frost.*

5. Obtain a *Peters Map* from Friendship Press and locate Seoul, Korea on the map. Discuss the way that the Pacific Basin and the countries of Asia look in comparison in size to the United States.

6. In your own view, how are the three resources for reflection discussed by Sano (scientific, biblical, and theological) related to each other in decisions about the meaning of your faith?

7. If you would like to discuss further the way the Korean context affects the questions asked about the Bible, read and discuss Letty Russell's short study book on Ephesians called *Imitators of God*.

Chapter 5: What Is Contextual Theology?

The purpose of chapter 5 is to introduce a way of doing theology that pays particular attention to how social, church, and theological contexts affect our thinking about life with God and neighbor. It raises the question for us of the bias of our own theological tradition and invites us to learn how to do theology in context.

1. Share examples with one another of your "most embarrassing moment" when you were caught with your bias or prejudice showing in something you said or did.

2. Remember that theological study does not have to be difficult when a group shares together in the discussion and helps to teach each other. If the group would like to continue further in discussion of contextual theology you can study Brown's *Theology in a New Key*.

3. Another way of learning to discuss theology together is to begin with the suggested steps in "A Model for Bible Study in Context." You might study one or more of the following passages: Luke 4:18–19; Luke 24:13–35; Jer. 29:10–14. These passages are introduced in chapter 1.

4. Bring copies of current newspapers to the group and have people pick out a news story and discuss how the story would be received differently by those who are rich/poor; black/white; male/female; gay or lesbian/straight; North American/Central American. If possible find examples of these different perspectives in reporting from different newspapers or magazines.

5. Attend a local antinuclear rally or discussion or demonstration and discuss how the social context of different people may affect the way they understand what God is calling them to do in regard to peacemaking.

6. Discuss Brown's contrast between Heb. 11:8b and 2 Cor. 4:7. Give examples of ways Christ remains the same while we keep needing new ways to explain who he is for us, and for others.

7. Having studied the material in this book, make your own list like that of Brown on ways of dealing creatively with faith in context.

A MODEL FOR BIBLE STUDY
IN CONTEXT

The purpose of this model is to suggest one way that small groups of persons can study the Bible together, emphasizing the learnings from this book on *Changing Contexts of Our Faith*. There are many ways of studying the Bible and it is important to make use of these different methods. This particular model is designed to help us learn more about the Bible and about our own faith by looking at how context shapes both the biblical message and our understanding of that message. It is also designed for small group interaction and, therefore, stresses sharing of questions and discussion after people have prepared themselves by studying the biblical text, as well as study guides and commentaries about the text. If everyone does not prepare ahead, at least the ones leading the study should have prepared the background of the text thoroughly.

The model is designed to stress the clues that were presented in the discussion of *Ways People Change* in the Introduction. It helps seek out new ideas and actions that might help us to grow in faith through noticing discord between our changing experience and the way we have been accustomed to think. It also encourages peer learning so that we can become theological resource persons for one another as we share together in teaching. The model itself is a continuing spiral of action/reflection that emphasizes the three clues for cultivating faithfulness in changing contexts.

Recognizing that all interpretation depends on the perspective of the interpreter, the model encourages us to listen to new voices of interpretation. Along with those of the experts and those in authority, it asks us to listen to those who have been voiceless because no one thought they had anything worthwhile to say. *Listening to the losers* not only brings new perspectives to our interpretation, it also brings us closer to the "least of our brothers and sisters," those whom Christ welcomed into the kingdom of

God (Matt. 25:31–46; 18:1–4). It is the marginal and suffering people of the earth who often speak to us in new ways about hope and faith and love if we take the time to listen carefully for their voices.

Recognizing that most of us learn by *acting our way into thinking* in new ways, the model invites us to participate fully in the discussion. This is a do-it-yourself study in which all need to take part and to risk discussion and new ways of acting, in order to find out what God is calling us to do in the changing context of our world. The first question in all three parts concerns reflections on our own actions and stories as a basis for listening to the text in our context. And a key aspect of the interpretation is testing out what we are learning through action in order to discern new clues to the meaning of a text and new questions to bring to the text.

Finally, recognizing that the biblical message itself has as one of its major themes "promise on the way to fulfillment," a third clue to this model of Bible study is that it emphasizes God's intended future. *Cultivating Advent Shock* as we approach the biblical text opens us up to ways that God might be calling us to act differently in the present as a sign of God's New Creation. It encourages us to look at the biblical texts in their own contexts and to be open to new questions and perspectives.

As we look at the basic model and then at illustrations of the model from a study of Exod. 1:8–2:10 it is important to remember that the study process is itself a spiral of interpretation through action/reflection and never reaches a conclusion. Instead it leads to some tentative clues and insights which in turn raise new questions and send us back to study the text over again. If a large group is engaged together in the study, it is possible to use this model by having small subgroups of two to four people who report back to the whole group at the end of Parts I, II, and III. If only a few people have studied in advance be sure to share background in the larger group.

Have people prepare in advance by reading the text, meditating on it, answering the questions in this outline, and reading commentaries or study guides if possible. The leader or leaders of the session need to do their homework as this model is not a substitute for exegesis, but rather a process for group study after the exegesis is completed. Begin the study with worship or prayer and read the Bible text aloud, providing time for everyone to meditate in silence on the text before beginning discussion. Allow two hours for the session.

1. *Listening to the Texts and Contexts to Find Questions that Open Up the Meaning of the Text.* Form into groups of two to four persons and discuss the three questions. Allow about forty-five minutes for this section, including the time to report back from the groups about the three questions. Reporting should include discussion of the background of the text (B), as well as the questions (C). On the basis of the questions shared, the group picks one question (from 1. C) that seems most likely to bring new insight to the particular text under study.

A. What is the setting or situation of your own life that most affects the way you see this text?
B. What is the setting or situation of the text that seems to have caused it to be spoken or written?
C. What would some person from a socially, economically, or physically disadvantaged group want to ask about this text?

2. *Sharing Stories in the Light of the Questions Asked.* After the group has selected the question (from 1. C) most likely to break open the meaning of the text in a new way, return to the small groups and discuss the next three questions. Allow forty-five minutes for discussion and reporting. If the group needs more direction, come back together after sharing A (the stories) and do B and C as a large group. If you have difficulty with stories from disadvantaged groups you might read parts of Ernesto Cardenal, *The Gospel in Solentiname.*

A. What stories or examples from your own experience can you share that help to bring the text and question alive?
B. What other biblical teachings or stories seem to echo or contradict the story or teaching of this text?
C. What stories do you know of persons from socially, economically, or physically disadvantaged groups that might bring a new perspective to the text?

3. *Searching for Clues that Emerge from Struggling with the Questions.* Because the spiral of interpretation continues, there are no conclusions in this study, but rather clues for further search and action or new questions that press for exploration. The clues are brief insights or "ah-ha's" that shed new light on the meaning of the text in the light of its context as well as our contemporary contexts. The clues are "serendipitous." That is, they happen unexpectedly as we listen to what others might be saying to us and reflect on our own actions and experiences. If you do not find any new clues the group can continue to discuss further exploration and options for actions of service. It is particularly helpful to plan for actions together and to include further reflection on the clues the following week when people share what happened next. This section takes about thirty minutes, but is often only "completed" in the reporting of the next session.

   A. What clue(s) for our own lives and actions have we discovered in studying the text together?
   B. What would you like to explore further about the clue(s) in this text or other related Bible texts?
   C. What can you do to test out your new understanding of the text in actions of service?

Examples of the Model from the Study of Exod. 1:8—2:10

This model is designed for use with a wide variety of biblical texts. For instance, an example of this method of contextual Bible study is found in Letty Russell, *Imitators of God*, which is a study book on Ephesians. Other examples are found in Robert McAfee Brown's book, *Unexpected News: Reading the Bible with Third World Eyes.* For the sake of illustration here I have chosen an Old Testament text which portrays the role of women as part of God's liberating actions on behalf of the Hebrew people. This text is well exegeted by Cheryl Exum: " 'You Shall Let Every Daughter Live': A Study of Exodus 1:8—2:10," *Semeia* 28 (1983): 113–26 and *Interpretation of the Bible*, ed. Letty Russell (Philadelphia: Westminster Press, 1985) 73–85. In giving examples for the model, I will be depending on her exegetical insights, but I will be giving experiences from my own life and context.

1. *Listening to Texts and Contexts to Find Questions that Open Up the Meaning of the Text.*

    A. What is the setting or situation of your life that most affects the way you see this text?

> My own personal experiences that bias my perspective are that I am an "uppity woman" interested in the stories of other women who defy Pharaoh. I taught Christian Education for many years and have always enjoyed teaching this story and found the stories of Moses especially exciting in the context of East Harlem in the 1960s as we struggled for Black Liberation.

    B. What is the setting or situation of the text that seems to have caused it to be spoken or written?

> The text is an introduction to the story of God's liberating action in the Exodus. These women are participants in this drama of the mighty acts of God. They seem to be included because of the usual patriarchal tradition that highlights the greatness of the hero by the story of miraculous birth. Yet the extraordinary courage shown by the midwives, Moses' mother and sister, Miriam, and Pharaoh's daughter demonstrate how God works through the courage and wit of those considered of "no account." The story of God's deliverence of the poor, the marginal, and the oppressed was a very important Israelite tradition.

    C. What would some person from a socially, economically, or physically disadvantaged group want to ask about this text?

> (1) Women would want to ask why they always get involved in the story as mothers but are seldom the major actors in biblical stories. (2) Those who are oppressed by dictatorships, poverty, or racism would want to know how God is at work in the world today to bring liberation.

2. *Sharing Stories in the Light of the Questions Asked.*

    A. What stories or examples from your own experience can you share that help to bring the text and questions alive?

> My own involvement in standing up to the U.S. government over issues of civil rights on behalf of black and Hispanic equal employment opportunity has led me to admire even more the great courage of people like those in South Korea who suffer torture and imprisonment on behalf of human rights and jus-

tice. As a woman I take courage from these women when I have to stand up to a "pharaoh" who controls my employment situation, or personal well-being.

B. What other biblical teachings or stories seem to echo or contradict the story or teaching of this text?

The story that seems most parallel is that of the women at the resurrection of Jesus Christ. Here also it is the women who have the courage to remain at the cross and to visit the tomb, thus becoming major participants in God's liberating action. There are parallels to many of the birth stories including that of Jesus. Attempts to condemn such "uppity behavior" when it disturbs the self-interest of male-dominated community life are seen in the story of Miriam's leprosy (Numbers 12) or in the condemnation of female leadership in the churches (Rev. 2:19–29).

C. What stories do you know of persons from socially, economically, or physically disadvantaged groups that might bring a new perspective to the text?

There are many stories of women who have the courage to stand up against the physical and verbal battering of their husbands in order to protect the lives of their children. (See Marie M. Fortune, *Sexual Violence*.) Often with the help of a battered women's shelter these women discover the courage to leave their husbands before they and their children are physically or emotionally destroyed. They are victims of the patriarchal myth that women can only exist as wives and mothers with someone to care for them even if that person is abusive. They are also examples of the courage mothers can display in going against religious, family, and social tradition to begin life anew.

3. *Searching for Clues that Emerge from Struggling with the Questions.*

A. What clues for our own lives and actions have we discovered in studying the text together?

My clue related to question 1 is that we need to *watch for the hidden message* in the biblical stories. This story assumes role stereotypes. It is no accident that women are featured in a birth narrative. The hidden message about a woman's "place" may be conveyed even when we rejoice in their "uppity behavior." My clue related to question 2 is that *courage happens when we use it.* Courage is a gift of God, but we only discover it in our own lives when we begin to act with courage. Then we are often amazed at our own gift of strength and caring. This is a clue to the way God is at work today bringing about liberation through the small but courageous actions of persons and groups that raise up signs of God's work of love and justice for all.

B. What would you like to explore further about the clues in this text or related texts?

> I would like to know more about Miriam's story as it is presently found in the Bible and as it might be reconstructed. I would also like to study the texts about the way God "hardens Pharaoh's heart" and how that relates to Pharaoh's stupidity in this story. (Phyllis Trible, *Texts of Terror*, or Elisabeth Schüssler Fiorenza, *In Memory of Her*, would be good to study in relation to reconstruction of women's stories.)

C. What can you do to test your new understanding of the text in actions of service?

> I would like to involve my local church in working more closely as volunteers and supporters of the local battered women's shelter. I would like to learn more about the effect of female and male stereotypes on the interaction of women and men in family situations. I plan to be more courageous in working for peace and human rights and against the pharaohs of our present world.

This interpretation would be far more rich and far more complex if a group of ten or twelve were all sharing out of their own contexts. There may be many clues and many ideas for action, but there will be no conclusion as the spiral of action/reflection on text and context continues.

ADDITIONAL RESOURCES

Billings, Peggy. *Fire Beneath the Frost: The Struggles of the Korean People and the Church.* Cincinnati: Friendship Press, 1984.

Bird, Phyllis A. *The Bible as the Church's Book.* Philadelphia: Westminster Press, 1982.

Brown, Robert McAfee. *Is Faith Obsolete?* Philadelphia: Westminster Press, 1974.

————. *Theology in a New Key: Responding to Liberation Themes.* Philadelphia: Westminster Press, 1978.

————. *Unexpected News: Reading the Bible with Third World Eyes.* Philadelphia: Westminster Press, 1984.

Brueggemann, Walter. *The Prophetic Imagination.* Philadelphia: Fortress Press, 1978.

Cardenal, Ernesto. *The Gospel in Solentiname.* 4 vols. Maryknoll, N.Y.: Orbis Press, 1982.

Casalis, Georges. *Correct Ideas Don't Fall from the Skies.* Maryknoll, N.Y.: Orbis Press, 1984.

Cone, James H. *My Soul Looks Back.* Nashville: Abingdon Press, 1982. Part of Journeys of Faith series, edited by Robert A. Raines and including volumes by Robert McAfee Brown, Rosemary Ruether, Virginia Mollenkott, and others.

Crotwell, Helen. *Women and the Word.* Philadelphia: Fortress Press, 1977.

Duck, Ruth C. and Michael G. Bausch, eds. *Everflowing Streams: Songs for Worship,* New York: Pilgrim Press, 1981.

Fiorenza, Elisabeth Schüssler. *In Memory of Her: A Feminist Reconstruction of Christian Origins.* New York: Crossroad, 1983.

Fortune, Marie M. *Sexual Violence: The Unmentionable Sin.* New York: Pilgrim Press, 1983.

Gonzalez, Justo L. and Catherine Gonzalez. *Liberation Preaching: The Pulpit and the Oppressed.* Nashville: Abingdon Press, 1980.

Huber, Jane Parker. *Joy in Singing.* Atlanta: Office of Women and The Joint Office of Worship, 1983. [341 Ponce de Leon Ave., N.E., Atlanta, GA 30365]

An Inclusive Language Lectionary: Readings for the Year A:B. National Council of Churches of Christ in the U.S.A. Atlanta: John Knox Press; New York: Pilgrim Press; Philadelphia: Westminster Press, 1983, 1984.

Koyama, Kosuke. *Waterbuffalo Theology.* Maryknoll, N.Y.: Orbis Press, 1974.

Loder, James E. *The Transforming Moment.* New York: Harper & Row, 1981.

Míguez-Bonino, Jose. *Faces of Jesus: Latin American Christologies.* Maryknoll, N.Y.: Orbis Press, 1984.

Mollenkott, Virginia R. *Women, Men and the Bible.* Nashville: Abingdon Press, 1977.

Niebuhr, H. Richard. *Christ and Culture.* New York: Harper & Brothers, 1951.

Peters, Arno. *Peters Map.* Cincinnati: Friendship Press, 1984. [P.O. Box 37844, Cincinnati, OH 45237]

Peters, Ted. *Fear, Faith and the Future: Affirming Christian Hope in the Face of Doomsday Prophecies.* Minneapolis: Augsburg Pub. House, 1980.

Ruether, Rosemary Radford. *Sexism and God-Talk: Toward a Feminist Theology.* Boston: Beacon Press, 1983.

———. ed. *Religion and Sexism.* New York: Simon & Schuster, 1974.

Ruether, Rosemary Radford and Eleanor McLaughlin. *Women of Spirit.* New York: Simon & Schuster, 1979.

Russell, Letty M. *Becoming Human.* Philadelphia: Westminster Press, 1982.

———. *Imitators of God: A Study Book on Ephesians.* Cincinnati: Service Center, General Board of Global Ministries, United Methodist Church, 1984. [7820 Reading Rd., Cincinnati, OH 45237]

———. ed. *Feminist Interpretation of the Bible.* Philadelphia: Westminster Press, 1985.

———. ed. *The Liberating Word.* Philadelphia: Westminster Press, 1976.

Sano, Roy I. *Outside the Gate: A Study of the Letter to the Hebrews.* Cincinnati: Service Center, General Board of Global Ministries, United Methodist Church, 1982. [7820 Reading Rd., Cincinnati, OH 45237]

Schaef, Ann Wilson. *Women's Reality: An Emerging Female System in the White Male Society.* Minneapolis, Mn.: Winston Press, 1981.

Soelle, Dorothee. *Choosing Life.* Philadelphia: Fortress Press, 1981.

Swartley, Willard. *Slavery, Sabbath, War and Women: A Casebook in Biblical Interpretation.* Scottdale, Pa.: Herald Press, 1983.

Tolbert, Mary Ann, ed. *The Bible and Feminist Hermeneutics. Semeia* 28. Chico, Calif.: Scholars Press, 1983.

Trible, Phyllis. *God and the Rhetoric of Sexuality*. Philadelphia: Fortress Press, 1978.

———. *Texts of Terror: Literary-Feminist Readings of Biblical Narratives*. Philadelphia: Fortress Press, 1984.

Whalberg, Rachel Conrad. *Jesus According to a Woman*. New York: Paulist Press, 1975.

———. *Jesus and the Freed Woman*. New York: Paulist Press, 1978.

Zikmund, Barbara Brown. *Discovering the Church*. Philadelphia: Westminster Press, 1983. Part of the Library of Living Faith, edited by John Mulder, with volumes by Letty M. Russell, Phyllis Bird, Gayraud S. Wilmore, and others.